HB
Tombstn Tx
Oct 2020

FORREST

MILITARY PROFILES
SERIES EDITOR
Dennis E. Showalter, Ph.D.
Colorado College

*Instructive summaries for general and expert
readers alike, volumes in the Military Profiles
series are essential treatments of significant and
popular military figures drawn from world history,
ancient times through the present.*

FORREST

The Confederacy's Relentless Warrior

Robert M. Browning Jr.

BRASSEY'S, INC.
Washington, D.C.

Library of Congress Cataloging-in-Publication Data

Browning, Robert M., 1955–
    Forrest : the Confederacy's relentless warrior / Robert M. Browning, Jr.—1st ed.
        p. cm. — (Military profiles)
Includes bibliographical references and index.
    ISBN 1-57488-624-X (hardcover : alk. paper) — ISBN 1-57488-625-8 (pbk. : alk. paper)
    1. Forrest, Nathan Bedford, 1821–1877. 2. Generals—Confederate States of America—Biography. 3. Confederate States of America. Army—Biography. 4. United States—History—Civil War, 1861–1865—Cavalry operations. I. Title. II. Series.

E467.1.F72B76 2003
973.7′3′092—dc21

                                                            2003012542

Hardcover ISBN 1-57488-624-X
Softcover ISBN 1-57488-625-8
(alk. paper)

Printed in the United States of America on acid-free paper that meets the American National Standards Institute z39-48 Standard.

Brassey's, Inc.
22841 Quicksilver Drive
Dulles, Virginia 20166

FIRST EDITION

10 9 8 7 6 5 4 3 2 1

To my parents

Robert Monroe Browning and
Barbara McElduff Browning

Contents

Maps

Preface

A lone Confederate cavalryman was fighting for his life. Surrounded by blue uniforms, the rebel horseman skillfully avoided the slashing sabers and gunfire. Shouts filled the air. "Kill him!" "Shoot him!" "Knock him off his horse!" The danger only made this sturdy cavalryman more determined. With his revolver, he began to open a path through the enemy troopers. Just as the soldier had nearly cleared the mass of Federal cavalry, one Union rider managed to discharge his carbine, the bullet lodging near the Confederate's spine. This wound would have incapacitated most men, but it only seemed to make the Confederate warrior do the extraordinary. Spurring his horse forward, he pulled a Union soldier up on his saddle to shield himself from further harm, and after riding out of danger, threw the man aside and rode to safety. This remarkable episode is just one of the many in the life of Nathan Bedford Forrest. During the Civil War, he personally killed thirty men and lost only one fewer horse in combat.

Not long after the Confederates had furled their flags for the last time, men began to write about Forrest. Many of his early biographers focused on this colorful and dashing figure, but he was an extremely complex man. He was a man of action, was often impetuous, but was always a leader of men. Throughout his life, his strong personality and his ability to deal quickly with difficult situations seemed to influence the outcome of every event in which he participated. His determination and decisiveness developed during his childhood on the frontier, and these traits served him well. He became a legend during his lifetime, and his enemies held him in both awe and fear.

This biography is an overview of Forrest—a survey of his life, his leadership style, and his military career. It is a starting place for further research. The scope of this book could never seriously scrutinize such a complex, controversial, and sometimes misunderstood figure. The many books that have examined him and his battles have yet to end the debate.

Certain moments create sparks for lifelong interest. The discussion on the merits of Forrest began for me during the spring of this nation's bicentennial. Dr. John Moseley strode across the front of his Civil War and Reconstruction class at the University of North Carolina at Wilmington. Discussing the cavalry actions in the Western Theatre, he spoke of Nathan Bedford Forrest and wove his exploits into the lecture. Moseley's eyes lit up, and with his tongue pressed hard into his cheek, he looked over his glasses toward his students and said, "Forrest was a mean un'. Yes, he was a mean un'." Dr. Moseley, thanks for the spark.

Others have assisted with this project. The interlibrary loan staff of the Prince William County library system was extremely helpful. Thanks also to my brother Bill, Mrs. Patricia LaPoint, Lyle Tate, Ron Brister, Gerald Counihan, Dr. Douglas Cupples, and the staffs of the National Archives, Duke University, and the Library of Congress. Scott Price, Chris Havern, and Bob Schneller deserve special thanks for their review of the manuscript. Lastly, my family and especially my wife deserve my thanks. They all shared their time with my work, and their love and support make my work possible.

1821	Forrest is born in Bedford County, Tennessee, on July 13.
1834	The Forrest family moves to Tippah County, Mississippi.
1841	In February Forrest joins a local militia unit to fight for the Republic of Texas.
1842	Forrest joins his uncle in business in Hernando, Mississippi.
1845	On March 9, Forrest is wounded in a street fight in Hernando, Mississippi. On September 25, he marries Mary Montgomery.
1851	Forrest moves to Memphis, Tennessee.
1858	Forrest is elected alderman in Memphis and is re-elected the following year.
1861	On June 14, Forrest enlists as a private in the Tennessee Mounted Rifles. In July, the governor requests him to raise his own cavalry unit. On October 26, Forrest is elected lieutenant colonel. On December 28, Forrest and his men fight their first major skirmish, at Sacramento, Kentucky.
1862	From February 14 to 16, Forrest helps defend Fort Donelson and then escapes before the fort is surrendered. The following month, he is elected colonel of the Tennessee Third Cavalry Regiment. On April 6–7, Forrest and his men fight at Shiloh and the following day at Fallen Timbers, where Forrest sustains his first wound of the war. On July 13, Forrest cap-

tures Murfreesboro, Tennessee. Eight days later, he is promoted to brigadier general. In a raid in western Tennessee, he fights at Lexington on December 18. On the 20th, he captures the Union garrison at Trenton, and on the 23d he captures the Federal garrison at Union, Tennessee. On December 31, he fights at the Battle of Parker's Crossroads.

1863 On February 3, Forrest and his men are repulsed at Dover, Tennessee. The following month, during operations in central Tennessee, Forrest fights at Thompson's Station on March 5, Brentwood on March 25, and Franklin on April 10. On April 23, Forrest begins his pursuit of Col. Abel D. Streight through northern Alabama forcing Streight's superior force to surrender on May 3. On June 13, Forrest is wounded by a disgruntled lieutenant, Andrew Wills Gould. On September 18–20, Forrest participates in the Battle of Chickamauga. On December 4, he is promoted to major general.

1864 In pursuit of Union Brigadier General William Sooy Smith, Forrest fights engagements at West Point, Mississippi, on February 21 and at Okalona the following day before Smith retreats. On April 12, Forrest captures Fort Pillow. The engagement becomes one of the most controversial battles of the war. On June 10, at Brice's Cross Roads, Forrest completely routs Brig. Gen. Samuel D. Sturgis in his most famous battle of the war. In July, Forrest tries to stop a Union column advancing into Mississippi. He fights Maj. Gen. Andrew Smith at Pontotoc on the 12th and at Tupelo on the 14th. On August 21, Forrest leads a daring raid on Memphis to prevent Smith from advancing farther into Mississippi during a second campaign. Forrest attacks Pulaski, Tennessee, on September 27 and on November 3 begins his siege of Johnsonville, Tennessee, which leaves the

Union depot in flames. At the end of November, Forrest supports Gen. John B. Hood's advance into middle Tennessee, fighting at Spring Hill on the 29th and at Franklin the next day.

1865   On February 28, Forrest is promoted to lieutenant general. He fights his last major battle, defending Selma, Alabama, on April 2.

1867   Forrest joins the Ku Klux Klan and is elected Grand Wizard.

1868   President Andrew Johnson pardons Forrest.

1869   Forrest orders the disbandment of the Ku Klux Klan.

1871   Forrest testifies before a congressional committee on the activities of the Klan.

1877   Forrest dies on October 29 in Memphis, Tennessee.

FORREST

Chapter 1

Frontiersman and Businessman

O N FRIDAY, JULY 13, 1821, twins cried out for the first time in a small rough-hewn frontier cabin in Bedford County, Tennessee. Born into poverty in the remote backwoods near the small village of Chapel Hill in middle Tennessee, only one of these children, Nathan Bedford Forrest, would live to adulthood. These circumstances of hardship and want did not limit him. Instead, they made him strong and provided him a foundation for later success.

Nathan was named after his grandfather, and his middle name, Bedford, came from the county of his birth. Bedford's grandfather moved the family to the Tennessee frontier from Orange County, North Carolina, in 1806. William Forrest, his father, was born around 1800 and married Mariam Beck in 1820. The family lived in a cedar cabin with a single room approximately eighteen by twenty feet with a loft for sleeping overhead. The Forrest family scratched out a living on a small patch of cleared land with a garden and an orchard. The house fronted the public road, and William Forrest, a blacksmith, built a shop across from his house. There he kept rudimentary tools of his trade and eked out a living for his growing family.

Bedford's formative years were spent in this cabin. His father and mother were both tall. William was more than six feet tall and was a sober, law-abiding, and industrious man. Mariam was nearly as tall as her husband and had a large frame. She was the ruling force in the household and raised her children strictly but affectionately.

In 1834 the Forrest family moved to Tippah County in northern Mississippi. They settled in a home on the banks of a small stream. Tragically, William died three years later, leaving Bedford, at age sixteen, as the head of the household. Young Forrest now had a responsibility to help support a widowed mother, six brothers, and three sisters, with another brother, Jeffery, born only four months later.[1]

Bedford's character was certainly influenced by his strong-willed and determined mother and the frontier society. Bedford would speak with pride about his teen years. Without his father, he and his brothers worked hard to clear land around their home and grew corn, oats, wheat, and cotton and raised livestock. They worked all day in the fields, and after sunset they kept busy making clothing and everything else the family needed. Forrest also recounted how he relied on the guidance of his mother.

Bedford met the challenges of the frontier and of raising a family the same way he met all his difficulties—directly and with vigor. There are numerous anecdotes of his formative years that illustrate how he dealt decisively with difficult situations and showed great courage and a strong will. One example will illustrate this. Bedford and a friend would occasionally ride their horses as a break from the routine of the farm. Many of these outings took the boys past a neighbor's cabin that was protected by two vicious dogs. The boys found great sport in luring the dogs to chase them with rocks, sticks, and taunts. One day the boys made their usual provocations, but when the dogs bounded toward the horses, Bedford's reared up and threw him off. Bedford sprang to his feet and readied himself for an attack, expecting to be torn apart by the hounds. Instead, the animals scampered back to the safety of the cabin. It is likely that these dogs saw in Bedford's countenance the same unflinching resolve that men would later see and also fear. Years after this event, Forrest admitted that it taught him that a bold attack could lead to success.

His determination and single-mindedness is best illustrated by the way he dealt with the dangers of the frontier. Shortly after his father's death, his mother and her sister rode to visit a distant neighbor. As the two were returning at dusk, a panther attacked them as their horses crossed a stream. The cat's front paws struck Mariam Forrest on the shoulder and neck while its back claws dug into the flanks of her horse. The horse bolted, and the panther fell off, ripping Mariam's clothing and inflicting deep lacerations. Hearing screams, Bedford rushed into the woods with his dogs, but the cat escaped. Determined to avenge his mother's wounding, he set out with his dogs and flintlock to kill the animal. He tracked the cat most of the night until the dogs treed it. Since it was too dark for him to get a good shot, he waited at the base of the tree until daylight. At dawn, he re-primed his gun and with one shot killed the cat, cut off its scalp and ears as a trophy, and returned home.

The challenges of the frontier continually confronted the young man. After his family moved to Mississippi, it was not too many years before other settlers began to claim the surrounding land. The Forrests' relationship with the family living on the farm next to them became unpleasant. The neighbor's ox continually broke through the fence on the Forrest property and damaged the corn and grain crops. Young Forrest asked his neighbor several times to put a yoke on the ox, with no result. Finally, he made an ultimatum. If the ox was found again inside his fence, he would shoot it.

A few days later, the ox was discovered on the Forrest farm and Bedford shot it. Hearing the report of the gun, the neighbor grabbed his rifle and hurried to deal with Bedford. Forrest, however, had quickly reloaded his flintlock and took a defensive stance at the fence between the properties. As his neighbor approached, Forrest said he wished him no harm but warned that he would kill him if he came closer. Bringing his gun up, he cocked the hammer and drew a bead on his neighbor. After considering the situation, the man realized that Bedford was serious, halted, and made no effort to cross the fence.

The rigors of the frontier also brought tragedy to the Forrest household. Typhoid fever took the lives of two of Forrest's brothers and all three of his sisters, including his twin, Fanny. Bedford's struggle with his environment and against poverty never allowed him the opportunity for a formal education. He spent a limited time at school but would never apply himself to his studies. He once expressed his dislike of school and writing by saying, "I never see a pen but what I think of a snake."[2]

In 1841 rumors of a potential Mexican attack on the Republic of Texas reached Mississippi. At the age of nineteen, Forrest joined a local military unit to fight for the Republic of Texas. He felt that his brothers, John and William, were old enough and his family was stable enough for him to leave home. In February he joined a company of men mustered in Holly Springs, Mississippi. They traveled to New Orleans, but their transportation to Galveston never arrived. At this point, many of the men in the company decided to return home. Forrest and a few of his company, however, made their way to Galveston to find that their services were not needed. They disbanded and made their separate ways home. Forrest was without funds and worked on a farm until he could raise enough money for his transportation back to Tippah County.

In 1842, Bedford accepted a business offer from his uncle in Hernando, Mississippi. He and his uncle speculated on horses and cattle. Bedford was successful and became wealthy. He earned a reputation as a sober, energetic, and honest businessman. In March 1845, a dispute between his uncle and a family of planters resulted in an altercation in the streets of Hernando. Forrest, not directly involved, arrived in town in time to intercept the men as they headed for his uncle's office. Forrest stopped them and told the four that he would not stand by while they attacked his aging uncle. If there were to be a fight, it would be a fair one, not four against one. One of the men drew a pistol and fired at Bedford, who returned fire. His uncle heard the gunshots, and when he entered the street he was mortally wounded by a bullet meant for his nephew. Forrest was slightly wounded but finished the fight by wounding three of the men and driving the last away. Forrest was charged and released; the other four were imprisoned.[3]

About six weeks later, he met his future wife, Mary Montgomery. While riding through the countryside on a Sunday morning, Bedford came across a carriage stalled in a creek. As he approached, he saw it contained two women, Mary Ann Montgomery and her mother. He also observed two men nearby on horseback watching the troubled carriage without offering their assistance. Bedford dismounted, hitched his horse to a fence, and waded through the mud and water to the carriage. He carried the two women across the creek and then used his large frame against the carriage to help the driver dislodge it from the mud. He then turned his attention to the two men. Forrest angrily admonished them for not helping the ladies and demanded they leave at once or he would give them a "thrashing they would never forget." That day he asked permission to call upon Miss Montgomery. After a short courtship, they married that September. The couple lived in Hernando in a modest double-log house covered with clapboards. Mary bore him two children, William Montgomery in 1846 and Frances A. (Fanny) in 1848, who lived only five years.

Bedford, getting restless and wishing to find other means to support his family, diversified his business. While still selling cattle and horses, he also began running a stage line from Hernando to Memphis, Tennessee; established a brickyard; and later began selling slaves. In 1849 his brickyard business went bankrupt after it suffered a huge loss in a single business venture.

In 1851 business opportunities appeared more favorable in Memphis, Tennessee. Bedford moved his slave business and his family to this booming river town. There he made his living sell-

*

ing real estate and slaves. Forrest was kind to his slaves and dressed and fed them well, as good business would dictate. He also refused to separate family members. In 1858, as a respected citizen, Forrest was elected alderman. He took his office seriously and always looked after the interests of the city. He continually found that he needed to protect Memphis from those politicians who sought to make a profit from their positions.[4]

By 1859 he had acquired much unclaimed cotton land and two plantations in Coahoma County, Mississippi. With these plantations yielding a large income, he closed his slave and real estate business in Memphis and devoted all of his time to his plantations.

Forrest owed his success to his hard work, strong will, and determination. Some thought him arbitrary and imperious. His language was sometimes violent and profane but never obscene or vulgar. Few, however, would ever challenge Forrest. He was nearly six feet two inches tall, weighed 180 pounds, and had broad shoulders and a large chest. His dark gray eyes often twinkled when he talked, yet when his temper flared his eyes changed his whole appearance. Instantly, those who saw this side of Forrest knew that they had better back away.

Forrest did well. In 1860, at thirty-nine, he had acquired holdings worth $1.5 million, a vast sum of money for the time. He had risen from poverty on the frontier to become one of the region's wealthiest men. Yet both Forrest and the nation were at a crossroads. Sectional crisis had troubled the United States for decades. Within a year, the country stood divided, and Forrest and his fellow Tennesseans would have to choose one of two paths, neither clearly delineated and both fraught with peril.

* THE HISTORY OF SLAVERY & CAPITALISM BOTH SUGGEST THAT THIS IS A DAMNED LIE EVERYTIME IT GETS PRINTED. SEE THE MYTH OF THE MERRY SLAVE.

Chapter 2

"First With the Most Men"

For DECADES sectionalism, slavery, economic rivalry, and cultural differences slowly but decisively cleaved the United States into two uncompromising camps. In 1860, Bedford Forrest stood to lose as much as any man. He had spent the previous ten years building a fortune and had become a prominent local figure. Forrest reflected the sentiments of many in the South. He was a states' rights Democrat who opposed secession and hoped a compromise could be reached. Beginning in December 1860, the Southern states began to secede one by one. The following April, after the bombardment and surrender of Fort Sumter, South Carolina, followed by President Abraham Lincoln's proclamation calling for troops, Forrest realized that sectional compromise was not possible. In June he put his business affairs in order and rode to Memphis to join the Confederate forces.[1]

Forrest reached Memphis with the intention of joining the Confederate units fortifying Randolph, Tennessee. Instead, on June 14, Forrest; his youngest brother, Jeffrey; and his fifteen-year-old son, William, enlisted as privates in Capt. Josiah S.

White's Tennessee Mounted Rifles. Less than one month later, however, Tennessee governor Isham G. Harris called Forrest to Memphis to raise a battalion of volunteer cavalry.[2]

Forrest received a commission as lieutenant colonel from the governor. He immediately placed a recruit notice in the Memphis *Daily Appeal* soliciting five hundred men to form a battalion of Mounted Rangers. He asked the recruits to bring their own mounts and arms—shotguns and pistols preferred. Understanding that the state would not be able to furnish the necessary equipment to outfit his unit, Forrest used his business contacts in Kentucky, northern Alabama, and Mississippi and managed to locate saddles, pistols, blankets, and other supplies. The operations to secure supplies in the neutral state of Kentucky were accomplished covertly. Southern sympathizers managed to procure sacks of pistols labeled as potatoes, and saddles labeled as leather and coffee.[3]

Members of the Boone Rangers, the first company mustered in his battalion, accompanied by many of their families, joined Forrest to escort the supplies back to Tennessee. Forrest met his first challenge when a local unit of Home Guards from Mumfordsville moved to intercept them. Fifteen miles out of Mumfordsville, Forrest decided to use a bluff, characteristic of many of his later engagements. He had his men, along with their family members, formed up in sight of the Louisville and Nashville Railroad tracks. As the train from Mumfordsville passed, he broke out the Confederate flag. The passengers on the train saw Bedford's swelled ranks. The reports that returned to the commander of the Union unit magnified the small command into a regiment. The Union force fled, and Forrest removed his supplies without a fight.[4]

Forrest drilled his men at the old fairgrounds in Memphis until all the companies were recruited. Forrest also brought along his slaves to serve as teamsters. Forty-seven in number, these men were promised their freedom when the war was over. By late October, Forrest had his command ready for action. Eight companies comprising about 650 men and described as "fine a body of men as ever went to the field" rode under his flag.[5]

Lieutenant Colonel Forrest proceeded with his men to Dover on the Cumberland River. Confederate forces had begun fortifying this point with a semicircular earthwork, later to be called Fort Donelson. A few days later, Forrest's battalion was ordered to Hopkinsville, Kentucky, and then on to Princeton to watch for enemy activity between the Cumberland and Green rivers.[6]

At Princeton, Forrest detached Maj. David C. Kelly to ride to the Ohio River to intercept Union shipping. Kelly, two companies, and a train of empty wagons started toward the river. Arriving at Ford's Ferry near Smithland at dark, they discovered a transport full of bacon, coffee, salt, and blankets tied up at the landing in the small town. Without making any noise, Kelly and thirty men boarded the cargo ship and captured the crew without a shot. At gunpoint Kelly and his men forced the crew to load the wagons with the supplies. As the heavily laden wagons crested the hill above the town, the Confederates set the ship afire. The mission was accomplished flawlessly and had one of the troopers boasting, "We were the proudest boys in the army."[7]

As Kelly and his men returned from Ford's Ferry, Forrest received word that the side-wheel gunboat USS *Conestoga* was steaming up the Cumberland River to Canton, reportedly to seize clothing destined for the Confederate Army. Forrest reacted quickly and took his entire battalion on a thirty-two mile, eight-hour night march to reach the town. He and his men reached the village just as the *Conestoga* hove into sight. Lt. Cmdr. S. Ledyard Phelps, the commanding officer of the *Conestoga*, immediately realized something was wrong because as he came to the landing in Canton, he noticed the inhabitants had fled. Phelps prepared his ship for action, and within moments Forrest's men opened up with small arms fire and a four-pound gun fired from a gully fifty yards from the gunboat. Phelps had his ship turned to use his stern gun. Clearing the woods with canister, he forced Forrest and his men to retreat from their masked position. Neither Forrest nor Phelps was willing to carry the engagement any farther, and both retired.[8]

Normally armies settle in camp during the winter months, yet

Forrest continued to make reconnaissance trips toward the Green River, northeast of Paducah, Kentucky. His command had increased to ten companies. Forrest took his relatively green troops into the field for a couple of weeks. On the day after Christmas, Forrest was ordered to determine if Union troops were moving north of the Green River at Hopkinsville. With about three hundred men, he began his trip in the mud and ice. On the 28th at Greenville, Kentucky, news reached him that a large Union force of about five hundred men was about eight miles north of them.[9]

When Forrest's men saw the enemy, he could not contain their enthusiasm and they began to race ahead. Forrest's command stretched out as the fastest horses outpaced the slower mounts. Near Sacramento, with Forrest at the head of the column, they met the Union rear guard. Forrest borrowed a Maynard rifle from one of his men and squeezed off the first shot. Forrest then ordered a charge. The Union rear guard rapidly rode toward the main force with Forrest's men in hot pursuit. With 150 of his men, he reached the Union forces drawn up at the crest of a wooded ridge. Moving forward, the Union cavalry opened with a sharp fire, and the Confederates returned it. Forrest realized that his men were still arriving on the field and halted his command. He then ordered them to fall back in hopes of drawing off the Union troops. This ploy worked, and the Federals rode after Forrest. When the slower Confederate cavalry finally arrived, Forrest dismounted some of his troops with Sharpe's carbines and Maynard rifles to act as sharpshooters. He then ordered flanking movements on both the right and the left and instructed the remaining men in the center to charge. The Union forces broke in confusion, and the rout began.[10]

Forrest and his men pressed the Union forces for three miles, shooting occasionally until they reached Sacramento. There they drew their sabers and began hacking at the rear of the Union force, leaving wounded Union troopers along the entire route. Forrest, still in the lead, overtook a private and shot him through the collar and with his sword mortally wounded a Union captain. The enemy, now in complete panic, began to throw down their weapons and made every attempt to escape. Major Kelly rode up to Forrest, who seemed "excited" and in a "desperate mood." Kelly later wrote, "His face was flushed till it looked like a painted warrior, and his eyes, usually mild in expression, glared like those of a panther about to spring upon its prey." Forrest's men killed sixty-five and wounded another thirty-five men of the enemy. This provided a glimpse of Forrest's style of combat, one that he would use time and again with success—envelopment by striking at the enemy's flanks, an attack from the front, and relentless pursuit.[11]

For several weeks, Forrest and his men performed scouting missions until ordered to report to Fort Donelson on the west bank of the Cumberland River. They arrived on February 10 to help defend this semicircular shallow earthen fort. Four days earlier, Union army forces consisting of fifteen thousand men under Brig. Gen. Ulysses S. Grant and a naval force under the command of Flag Officer Andrew Hull Foote, had approached Fort Henry on the Tennessee River only twenty miles to the west of Fort Donelson. Confederate Brig. Gen. Lloyd Tilghman, who had only 3,400 men and 17 antiquated cannon to defend the fort, sent all but about 100 of his men to Fort Donelson. Tilghman and his outmatched force fought the Federal gunboats for a short while and then surrendered. Fort Donelson now stood in the way of the Union forces' ability to control the Tennessee and Cumberland rivers and turn Gen. Albert Sidney Johnston's positions in Kentucky. Brig. Gen. John B. Floyd commanded the fort with Maj. Gen. Gideon J. Pillow and Brig. Gen. Simon Bolivar Buckner also there.

On February 12, Forrest moved forward to observe the Union approach. They checked the advance guard of the Union army for several hours before returning to the fort. The following day, both sides skirmished as the Union forces began to envelop the fort. On the afternoon of the 14th, Foote's small flotilla reached Fort Donelson and put the Confederates under fire, despite effective and damaging fire from the Confederate guns. Forrest and Kelly, a reverend before the war, rode to the river to see the naval bombardment. Witnessing the intense duel, Forrest shouted above the exploding shells, "Parson! For God's sake, pray; nothing but God Almighty can save that fort!"[12]

The Confederate generals held a council of war on the night of the 14th. During the day the fort's batteries had successfully kept the Union gunboats at bay. Two of the Union warships had lost their steering and floated downstream, and Foote had withdrawn. Floyd, however, believed he could not hold the fort and determined to attack the Federal right flank and escape southward along the river.

Early on the 15th, the Confederates including Forrest and his command rushed the complacent Federal troops and surprised them. Forrest's men fought for two hours and pushed the enemy back, but he was unable to flank the Union positions. The rebel infantry continued to push the Union forces away from the fort, and as they retreated in haste, Forrest and his cavalry advanced past the infantry. Later that morning, he charged and captured a battery of six guns that had checked the Confederate forces for some time. The Union forces were beginning to lose cohesion, and General Pillow rode up to Forrest and ordered him to charge down a ravine. Forrest drove the enemy out, "leaving 200 in the hollow, accomplishing what three different regiments had failed to do." His men captured three more guns and killed fifty sharpshooters protecting these guns.[13]

At 2:30, Pillow ordered a halt after the Confederates had pushed the Union forces back for miles and had opened three roads for escape. During the day, Forrest lost about 350 men, who were killed, captured, and wounded. Two horses were killed under him during the battle; the first had seven wounds and fell dead from loss of blood. The second died when an artillery shell struck it just under the saddle skirt, barely missing Forrest and making his legs numb from the shock.[14]

After opening this escape route, Pillow inexplicably ordered his forces to withdraw to the fort. That evening near midnight, another council of war among the three Confederate generals ended in a decision to surrender. But neither General Pillow nor General Floyd wished to make the capitulation and escaped in boats, leaving this unpleasant task to the junior general, Simon Buckner.

Forrest, however, refused to surrender his battalion and expressed his utter dissatisfaction with the decision. At 4:00 A.M., he moved out by a road he had scouted the day before. With five hundred of his men and about two hundred from other units, Forrest escaped without a shot being fired and rode toward Nashville. Later that morning, General Buckner asked for terms of surrender from Grant, who insisted on unconditional surrender.[15]

Before noon on the 18th, Forrest and his horsemen arrived at the outskirts of Nashville, and he halted his worn-out troops. The city's inhabitants were already in a state of panic due to the fall of the forts. Forrest rode into town to report to Gen. Albert Sydney Johnston, who directed Forrest to report to General Floyd. Floyd was in charge of removing the valuable public property from the town before it was abandoned. Forrest was given command of the city and was ordered to patrol it until the next afternoon before joining Floyd in Murfreesboro. Forrest found that all but one officer from the commissary and quartermasters departments had fled, leaving the depot open to plundering mobs. Forrest ordered his troops to draw their sabers and clear the rabble. After securing the depot, Forrest rode away to determine the situation in other parts of the city. Shortly after leaving, he learned that a mob had returned and broken into the depot again. Forrest returned to the scene, where a man rushed him and seized him by the collar, exclaiming his right to the government supplies. Forrest pulled his revolver and clubbed the man, sending him screaming with pain back into the street. The Confederate troopers again cleared the depot, only to have the crowd make a third attempt. Forrest finally used a steam fire engine to hose down the mob with ice-cold water. They did not return.[16]

On Friday the 21st Forrest sent most of his men to Murfreesboro while he stayed to supervise the removal of stores and ammunition by rail, wagons, carts, and drays. He was able to save 700 boxes of clothing, about 750 wagonloads of meat (250,000 pounds), and 40 wagonloads of ammunition. The advance column of Union Brig. Gen. Don Carlos Buell's army arrived on the outskirts of Nashville at 11 A.M. on the 23rd, and Forrest and his small detachment of men rode to Murfreesboro.[17]

This episode reveals much about Forrest. When those around him panicked and fled, Forrest remained calm and offered solutions. He showed an ability to assess the situation and deal forcefully to resolve problems. His high energy and strong personality also helped to keep those around him focused and, like their leader, unaffected by the confusion that paralyzed the Confederate leadership. Forrest was extremely critical of the quartermasters and commissary departments and reported that had they "remained at their post and worked diligently . . . the Government stores might all have been saved."[18]

After reporting to General Johnston in Murfreesboro, Forrest and his troops were sent to Huntsville, Alabama, to refit and for a furlough. At Huntsville, Forrest's battalion was reorganized into a regiment. A new company under the command of his brother Jesse joined the unit, which now became the Tennessee Third Cavalry Regiment under the command of the newly elected Colonel Forrest.[19]

The fall of forts Henry and Donelson opened middle Tennessee to a Union invasion and changed the strategic situation in the west. While Buell occupied Nashville, General Grant penetrated deeper into Confederate territory by taking his troops up the Tennessee River and landing on the west bank at Pittsburg Landing. Buell and Grant envisioned a coordinated attack on the Confederate railhead at Corinth, Mississippi, twenty-three miles south of Grant's camp. Confederate general Johnston, who was at Corinth, however, decided to strike Grant before Buell could join him. The Confederates left Corinth on April 3, expecting to arrive the following day. Thick woods, rain, and poor roads delayed Johnston's men, and they were not ready to attack the Union positions until the afternoon of the 5th. Despite the fact that the Confederates had not approached stealthily, Grant was unprepared for an attack.

On the 6th, a heavy mist hung over Shiloh Church when, at 5 A.M., Confederate skirmishers opened fire on the Union positions. Forrest's regiment had advanced with the army, but was halted toward the rear to guard the fords across Lick Creek on the Confederate right and to watch for the enemy farther south. At 11:00 he received orders to move his regiment to the front. Before riding forward, Forrest assembled his men and addressed them. He said, "Boys, do you hear that musketry and that artillery? It means that our friends are falling by the hundreds at the hands of the enemy and we are sitting here guarding a damned creek! Let's go and help them."[20]

At a gallop Forrest moved his men to the sound of the heaviest fighting, which meant he passed from the right flank toward the center of the Confederate line. He found Brig. Gen. Frank Cheatham trying to break through at the Hornet's Nest. Impatiently he rode up to Cheatham and asked if his men could join in the charge across an open field to their front. Cheatham would not give orders to Forrest, feeling that his mounted men would be conspicuous targets. Forrest, however, was determined to fight. Forming his men into columns of four, he gave the order to charge. Forrest's men rapidly covered the ground between them and the Union lines, and several men and horses fell to Union fire. Forrest's men, however, were stopped by a marsh about a hundred feet in front of the Federal lines. Cheatham followed Forrest's movement with his troops and drove the Union forces back. Forrest's men, meanwhile, made a detour around the swamp and attacked the Federal lines, which were now in a confused mass and heading toward the river.[21]

It was at this point in the battle that the Confederate onslaught began to falter. Early in the afternoon, a bullet struck an artery in General Johnston's leg, and in less than an hour he was dead. Command of the army fell on the shoulders of Gen. Pierre Gustave Toutant Beauregard. The surviving Union troops in the Hornet's Nest were finally overwhelmed and surrendered, but by delaying the Confederate attack on the right they had allowed Grant to solidify his defensive position and mass artillery at the landing on the river. The Confederates, contented with the hard-won ground and the arms, ammunition, and other supplies they had captured, rested for the night.

Forrest had taken part in only a small portion of the day's fighting, and that night he sent out his scouts. They witnessed the Union army in complete chaos with reinforcements arriving by the river. Forrest sent messages to his superiors that if they attacked, they might drive the Federal forces into the river. Getting no response, Forrest mounted his horse and rode to the nearest corps headquarters. There he found Maj. Gen. William J. Hardee and Brig. Gen. John C. Breckinridge. Forrest relayed the information from his scouts and insisted the army attack or withdraw before the Union could mass its troops. Hardee recommended that he communicate with Beauregard, so Forrest rode off to find him. Unable to find Beauregard in the darkness, he rode back to his men and sent another scouting party forward. They returned with the same information as before. Forrest rode again to relay this information. At the headquarters he met Brig. Gen. James R. Chalmers. Forrest told Chalmers, "If the enemy come on us in the morning, we will be whipped like hell." Forrest was, however, instructed to return to his unit.[22]

The Union forces, greatly strengthened during the night, took the offensive Monday morning. The first advance by the enemy took place just before daybreak, toward Forrest's position. His men, many of whom were clothed in captured Union cavalry coats, deceived the Union pickets and captured fifty enemy soldiers. At 5:30 the Federal skirmishers were pushed out in force and Forrest slowly fell back until 7:00, when General Hardee directed him to retire.[23]

The now outnumbered Confederates fought stubbornly through most of the day as they fell back toward Corinth. Late in the afternoon, Beauregard ordered his army to retreat. Forrest's regiment remained on the right flank and kept stragglers to a minimum. On the night of the 7th, Forrest picketed on the right to prevent the Union forces from surprising the retreating Confederates.[24]

On Tuesday morning, while performing rear-guard duty, Forrest found himself facing two battalions of cavalry and a Union regiment across two hundred yards of felled trees from a prewar logging effort. As the Union forces advanced across the ground, they became disorganized, and when they crossed a stream Forrest recognized that they were at a real disadvantage. With only about 350 men, 150 of whom were supported by infantry from Texas and a Kentucky cavalry unit, he decided to attack. The bugler sounded the advance, and after a volley from the Confederates, the Union troops began to withdraw. The retreat, however, soon turned into a rout, and the Union cavalry rode over its own infantry to escape. Forrest's men closely pursued it for several hundred yards and rode down on the hapless Union infantry left behind, inflicting heavy casualties.[25]

Forrest, in his excitement, however, rode beyond his own men and found himself amid the enemy cavalry. His men had stopped to collect their prisoners and then had fallen back. The Federal cavalry and soldiers began firing at Forrest, while yelling, "Kill him!" "Shoot him!" "Stick him!" "Knock him off his horse!" Shots began to strike his horse as Forrest cleared a path with his revolver through his assailants' slashing sabers and flashing guns. One Union rider managed to close in on Forrest and discharged his rifle into the colonel's side. The bullet entered above his left hip, lodged by his spine, and numbed his leg. Forrest knew he had to escape, and as he rode away he pulled a small Union soldier onto his saddle behind him to shield his back. When he had ridden a safe distance, he dropped the man and continued toward his lines. Forrest went to the nearest surgeon, who could not find the ball and gave the opinion that the wound might be fatal. Forrest continued to Corinth, but the pain became so unbearable that he dismounted and rode in a buggy for the remaining miles. The skirmish at Fallen Timbers checked Brig. Gen. William Tecumseh Sherman's advance on the Confederate rear. Sherman wrote that Forrest's men broke through his line of skirmishers and that they "without cause, broke, threw away their muskets, and fled."[26]

Forrest was furloughed for sixty days to recuperate in Memphis. His hardy constitution, however, had him seemingly well enough at the end of April to return to his command. While Forrest was in the saddle, performing a reconnaissance during Maj. Gen. Henry Halleck's siege of Corinth, his horse jumped over a log and reopened the wound. In agony, Forrest had the bullet extracted and took two more weeks to recuperate in Memphis.[27]

During his recuperation, Forrest remained busy. Since he had mustered the first company of his battalion in the fall of 1861, Forrest and his men had actively engaged the enemy, causing a loss through battle and disease of nearly half of the command. With only three hundred effectives, Forrest, never one for inactivity, began to advertise for recruits. His advertisement asked for men who wanted to be "actively engaged" and concluded, "Come on, boys, if you want a heap of fun and to kill some Yankees."[28]

Forrest hurried back to his regiment as soon as he could ride again. Near Corinth, Mississippi, in one of the small actions between Halleck's army and Beauregard's, Forrest again showed his ability to confuse and thoroughly rout his opponent. The engagement is best summed up in a letter from Bedford to his friend D. C. Trader. Indicative of Forrest's poor command of grammar, he wrote, "I had a small brush with the Enamy [sic] on yesterday. I suceded in gaining their rear and got into thir entrenchments . . . and Burned a portion of thir camp. . . . They wair not looking for me I taken them by suprise they run like Suns of Biches."[29]

In June, just as the new recruits began to report for duty, Forrest was ordered to Chattanooga to assume command of another cavalry unit. With regret he left the Third Tennessee Regiment behind except for a small group of handpicked staff, including his brother William. Pulling together his diverse unit with troops from Texas, Georgia, Tennessee, and Kentucky, was a challenge. Bedford put his usual energy into his new command and had them ready to advance on the enemy after a month of training.[30]

After the loss of western Tennessee, the Confederates wished to stop or stall the advance of Buell's Army of the Ohio into middle Tennessee. Both Maj. Gen. Braxton Bragg, the new commander of the Confederate Army of Mississippi, and Beauregard hoped that an aggressive thrust might halt Buell. Enlisting the help of Maj. Gen. E. Kirby Smith's army, near Knoxville, Bragg planned to move north while Smith crossed the Cumberland Mountains. The combined armies would strike Buell's forces in Kentucky near the Ohio River.

Before all this could be put into motion, they sent Forrest to capture Murfreesboro, Tennessee. On July 9, Forrest pushed his command of a thousand men across the Tennessee River. On a forced march of sixty miles, they took two routes toward McMinnville with Murfreesboro as the final destination. Arriving at McMinnville on the 11th, Bedford and his men rode an additional fifty miles to the outskirts of Murfreesboro. Forrest sent in a company of Col. John A. Wharton's Texas Rangers who bluffed their way past the sentinels and then captured all of them without firing a shot.[31]

Without hesitation Forrest decided to attack. Forrest was able to capitalize on a feuding Federal garrison that had split itself on opposite sides of the town. His entire force would ride quickly and at the outskirts of Murfreesboro split into four groups, one held in reserve for support. Wharton's Texans would take the lead and engage the main enemy camp and capture them or at least isolate them from the rest of the fighting. The second group, under Forrest, would ride into town, and the third would ride to the opposite side of Murfreesboro to engage Union units on that side and cut off any retreat.[32]

The attack, however, failed to develop as expected. Wharton led his Texans down the macadamized turnpike without waiting for the proper signal. Additionally, some of Wharton's men followed the main body of cavalry into the town, leaving him only about two hundred troopers. Wharton, riding boldly down on the Union position, arrived at the Federal camp before the other Confederate units were deployed. Surprising the garrison,

Wharton's men initially caused confusion in the encampment with their shotguns and pistols, but the enemy rallied. Wharton was seriously wounded, and the Federal units put up a defensive barrier using overturned wagons and other cover. Unable to carry the position, Wharton fell back and remained engaged until Forrest could later come up.[33]

Forrest, who often started his men into battle with the command "Forward, men, and mix with 'em!," rode at the head of the column striking into the town. After more than two hours of fighting, he captured the courthouse, the telegraph office, and the jail, along with Union Brig. Gen. Thomas Crittenden and his staff. The Confederate troops attacking the far camp came under a tremendous artillery fire and failed to capture this position. Forrest later rode his force into the enemy's rear and burned the camp and its stores. After fighting for nearly six hours, Forrest and his men finally secured all but the position Wharton had failed to carry earlier. Forrest sent a message demanding unconditional surrender or he would "have every man put to the sword." After a short parlay, the Federal troops surrendered.[34]

On his birthday, Forrest captured more than 1,100 men, 4 pieces of artillery, more than 50 large wagons and their teams, cavalry, horses, equipment, 1,200 stand of arms, and 30,000 uniforms. The Confederates lost twenty-five killed and sixty-six wounded, while the Federal losses were reported to be about twenty-five killed and more than one hundred wounded. Gen. Basil Duke, some years after the victory at Murfreesboro, asked Forrest how he succeeded in such a brilliant victory. Forrest said, "I just took the short cut and got there first with the most men."[35]

Forrest, ever diligent, knew that the nearby Federal garrisons might still be concentrated against his force. He gave orders to destroy all the Union supplies that could not be carried off and by 6:00 P.M. had his men on the road back to McMinnville. He ordered units to destroy bridges and scout Union positions for movement. Forrest also carried off his Union prisoners despite advice from his officers to leave them. He said, "I did not come here to make half a job of it; I am going to have them all."[36]

With zeal, Forrest five days later took seven hundred men on reconnaissance toward Nashville. With rapid movements in a semicircle around Nashville, he captured pickets and small enemy detachments, burned bridges, cut telegraph wires, and burned a "considerable amount of stores" at the Antioch Depot. He captured nearly a hundred prisoners and killed and wounded another two dozen without the loss of a man. Leaving the city in confusion, he rode back to McMinnville.[37]

Buell considered these attacks "disgraceful" and sent Brig. Gen. William Nelson in pursuit of Forrest. Nelson boasted, "Mr. Forrest shall have no rest. I will hunt him myself." Nelson, with about three thousand infantry, quickly moved to engage Forrest, but Forrest merely led his men just off the turnpike, let Nelson pass, and then continued to safety. Nelson countermarched and pursued, and again Forrest turned his troops off the main road and let the enemy pass. Forrest left Nelson's footsore and tired soldiers covered in dust as he rode back to McMinnville. Nelson gave up on July 30, writing that he could not chase Forrest's cavalry "mounted on race horses" with his infantry in the hot weather.[38]

On September 3, Forrest reported to Gen. Braxton Bragg in Sparta, Tennessee. Here Bragg transferred the four Alabama companies of his old regiment back to Forrest. As Bragg moved his army into Kentucky in order to join Kirby Smith and secure the state for the Confederacy, Forrest followed, reaching Glasgow on the 10th. He was temporarily detached to Maj. Gen. Leonidas Polk's Army of Mississippi. Advancing to Polk's headquarters at Bardstown, Forrest received a communication asking him to report again to Bragg. In late September, he was directed to turn over his brigade to Colonel Wharton, travel to Murfreesboro, establish a new headquarters, and recruit another brigade. He was allowed to take his old Alabama regiments and his staff. On July 21, during his lightning forays against the enemy, Forrest had been promoted to brigadier general.

Chapter 3

"All Is Fair in Love and War"

F ORREST'S EASY CAPTURE of Murfreesboro should have demonstrated his value as a leader and field commander. Yet Bragg decided to again take him from the field and turn him into a recruiter. Forrest established his headquarters at Murfreesboro and had no trouble raising regiments for active service. Many of the new recruits, however, had only shotguns and squirrel rifles they had brought from home. The issued weapons were little better and included flintlock muskets.[1]

Forrest, now a general officer, might have found it difficult to administer his larger command. While Forrest was intelligent, he certainly never had the education to perform administrative tasks, particularly correspondence, with ease or efficiency. He relied on his adjutants. Officers like Maj. John P. Strange helped him to write and polish his communications. Yet sometimes Forrest's rough-hewn personality could not be contained. During the war, one of his men requested a furlough twice, and twice Forrest refused the request. When the application came across Forrest's desk a third time, he wrote on the request, "I told you twist [twice] Goddammit know."[2]

In six weeks, Forrest had three regiments of Tennessee cavalry and his old Fourth Alabama Cavalry regiment strengthened by an additional six companies and a battery of artillery, all organized into a brigade. When Maj. Gen. John C. Breckinridge assumed command of all the troops in the area and moved to Murfreesboro, Forrest moved his men northwest to La Vergne. Bragg, however, then placed Forrest's brigade under the command of Gen. Joseph Wheeler. Ostensibly Forrest maintained an independent command, doing what he did best, raiding the enemy's supply lines.

Winter operations were difficult at best, and Forrest struck out with green and inadequately armed troops. Crossing the Tennessee River, he rode toward Lexington, Tennessee. Here on December 18, he met eight hundred Federal troops supported by artillery. After a short and sharp fight, Forrest drove the Union troops off the field and captured nearly 150 men and large amounts of supplies, ammunition, and weapons, including two three-inch Rodman guns.[3]

The next morning he pushed west toward Jackson. He hoped to reach the Mobile and Ohio Railroad and the Memphis and Ohio Railroad to sever Grant's north-south and east-west supply lines. Forrest split his forces and sent some toward Corinth and others toward Bolivar to burn trestles and bridges while other troops destroyed stations and tracks.

News of Forrest had the Union leadership frozen in panic. Some estimated Forrest's 2,500 men to be nearly ten times that large. Forrest, though, with cunning had released prisoners with disinformation. He also cultivated the illusion of a larger command—one of his trademarks. He marched in sight and sound of the enemy, his men beating kettledrums to imitate marching infantry.[4]

At dawn on the 19th, Forrest moved with a portion of his men to Jackson, and the Union garrison withdrew into the town's fortifications. Playing havoc with the rail lines, Forrest left the next day, leaving only a small force of skirmishers behind to keep the enemy at bay while he rode north to Humbolt. There he captured the garrison and its supplies. Riding north to Trenton on the afternoon of the 20th, the Confederates met a withering fire from the Union garrison, but Forrest brought up his artillery, and after the third round was fired, the garrison of seven hundred surrendered. The Confederates also captured a substantial amount of commissary and quartermasters stores.[5]

On the morning of the 21st, after destroying the government property he could not carry away, his force continued northward to Union City. Forrest and his men destroyed bridges and rails as they went and captured Union solders who guarded the strategic points. On the 23d, he rode into Union City and captured the 106-man garrison without firing a gun. On Christmas morning, Forrest guided his men southeast toward Dresden, leaving a path of destruction as they rode along the Nashville and Northwestern Railroad. By this time the Union leadership had ample opportunity to concentrate their forces, and Brig. Gen. Jeremiah C. Sullivan had men moving from three different directions.[6]

Forrest and 1,800 men continued southeast toward McKenzie and McLamoresville, crossing the Mobile and Ohio Railroad. Forrest successfully evaded the Union forces with careful reconnaissance and movement. While camped near Parker's Crossroads on the night of December 30, his brother Capt. William Forrest discovered two Union brigades nearby.

Before dawn the Union troops under Col. Cyrus L. Dunham and Forrest began to move toward the crossroads. At 9 A.M. Forrest met Dunham with two regiments supported by artillery. The Confederates attacked and forced the Union line to withdraw to a stronger position at a split-rail fence. Keeping his artillery forward, Forrest hoped to push the Federal troops off the field without fully committing his cavalry. True to form, Forrest split his forces to strike at the enemy's flanks. The Union troops now advanced but were repulsed by the Confederate artillery. After noon, as Dunham's troops withdrew, Forrest ordered a charge and the Union line disintegrated. In the chaos the Confederate cavalry struck the rear of the Union lines, capturing the supply train.[7]

Forrest wrote, "We drove them through the woods with great

slaughter and several white flags were raised in various portions of the woods and the killed and wounded were strewn over the ground." Forrest immediately asked for unconditional surrender, and Dunham refused. Before Forrest had time to consider his next move, to his astonishment, another battle erupted to his rear. In disbelief Forrest rode to the sound of the guns to confirm that the Union forces were to his rear. The second Union brigade, under Col. John W. Fuller, was now attacking with vigor, and Forrest was met by a stampede of horses and horse holders in the rear of his dismounted men.[8]

During this crisis Forrest remained calm. One of his staff officers reportedly came up for instructions. "General . . . What shall we do? What shall we do?" he asked. Forrest's reply was, "Charge them both ways." Forrest's troops abandoned the captured supply train and three captured guns, reversed front, fought their way through Dunham's confused troops, and withdrew southward. Forrest took with him three hundred Federal prisoners, which offset the approximately three hundred dismounted Confederate troops he had lost when Fuller stampeded their tethered horses. Forrest's forces suffered about sixty killed and wounded, and the Federals 27 killed and 140 wounded. This battle illustrated Forrest's talent for making quick decisions and changing his tactics in the face of impending disaster.[9]

Forrest crossed the Tennessee River at Clifton at noon on New Year's Day. His men had traveled about twenty miles a day during their fifteen-day foray into west Tennessee. They had netted about 2,500 prisoners, 50 wagons, 10,000 stand of arms, 1 million rounds of ammunition, blankets, and other supplies. They had destroyed about fifty trestles and bridges, burned about twenty stockades, and taken or disabled ten pieces of field artillery. His men crossed a river seven hundred yards wide using skiffs, while pressed by an enemy four times his number. Despite his battlefield losses, he returned with new recruits—his command stronger in number than when he began.[10]

Forrest moved his brigade to Columbia, Tennessee, where his men rested and refitted. Here he anchored Bragg's left flank. The three-day Battle of Stone's River, which began on December 31, 1862, convinced Bragg to withdraw toward Shelbyville.

Wheeler was now ready to use Forrest to interrupt Union commerce on the Cumberland River. Wheeler decided to attack the Union post at Dover, just upstream from Fort Donelson. The Confederate forces arrived at Dover at about 12 noon on February 3, with plans to overcome the garrison quickly by rushing it from both sides. Forrest protested against this attack but was ordered forward nevertheless. He and eight hundred men took the right flank for a coordinated assault at 2:30 that afternoon. Confederate artillery opened the engagement. Before Wheeler and his men could get into position, Forrest observed some Federal troops marching at a double quick toward the river. Thinking the garrison was trying to escape, Forrest ordered a charge. The movement, however, was merely an effort by the fort's commander to reposition some troops in a ravine.[11]

Forrest, leading his men, rode at full speed toward the trenches. The Confederates met a deadly fire from the Union garrison. A thirty-two-pounder mounted in the fort, double-shotted with canister, caused carnage. Forrest's horse was shot and fell just short of the guns, throwing the general to the ground. His men believed him dead and withdrew under fire. Forrest, however, quickly rejoined his men to reorganize them for another assault.[12]

Forrest remounted to lead his now dismounted men against the enemy. They drove the Union soldiers out of some houses near the fort, but again they failed to carry the Union lines. Forrest lost a second horse and injured himself this time when he fell. The Confederates on the left, led by Brig. Gen. John Wharton, however, succeeded in breaking through the outer defenses. But night had fallen, they had exhausted their ammunition, and they had to withdraw. In the battle, Forrest lost about a fourth of his men. Forrest, Wheeler, and Wharton met and decided the Union positions were too strong.[13]

Bedford Forrest did not take failure well and he brooded for hours after the attack. At the headquarters later that night, General Wharton dictated his report to one of his aides with both Forrest and Wheeler also by the fire. Wharton said something that touched a nerve in Forrest, and he interrupted the dictation. Forrest, perhaps still hurting from his earlier fall, in an angry and excited tone said, "I have no fault to find with my men. In both charges they did their duty as they have always done." Wheeler interjected to appease Forrest by saying, "General Forrest, my report does ample justice to yourself and to your men." Forrest, however, could not contain his anger and now struck out at Wheeler. Forrest replied, "General Wheeler, I advised against this attack, and said all a subordinate officer should have said against it, and nothing you can now say or do will bring back my brave men." He continued, "I mean no disrespect to you; you know my feeling of personal friendship to you; you can have my sword if you demand it; but there is one thing I do want you to put in that report to General Bragg—tell him I will be in my coffin before I will fight again under your command."[14]

Despite this quarrel, both men continued their friendship and served on the opposite flanks of Bragg's army until Confederate president Jefferson Davis gave Forrest his own command. It showed, however, Forrest's continuing independence and self-reliance. The traits he had acquired on the frontier as a child produced a good leader but not a follower.

On the morning of February 4, the battered Confederates withdrew from Dover. Forrest's men occupied their old quarters at Columbia for several weeks. Bedford reorganized and drilled his men so that when they took the field again they would be better prepared.

In early February, Maj. Gen. Earl Van Dorn arrived in middle Tennessee with three brigades of cavalry to help guard the left flank of the Army of Tennessee. The Confederates kept picket lines near the enemy's forces in Franklin. On the night of March 4, scouts returned with intelligence that the enemy was on the move southward.

On 5 March, Forrest and the Confederates deployed near Thompson's Station and awaited the Federal forces. Forrest divided his men, and while two of his regiments attacked the Union front and flank, the general took the rest of his men to attack the enemy rear. The Federal force did not panic, and Forrest charged twice, losing another horse in the first charge and leading a second charge on foot. During the second attack, he broke through the Union line and cut off the enemy's line of retreat. The Confederates captured more than 1,200 men and the Union supply train. Van Dorn lost 357 casualties, and the Union forces, in addition to those captured, suffered another 300 killed and wounded. This battle reinvigorated Forrest and his men, who were "eager for an opportunity to wipe out the disappointment of Dover."[15]

The Union forces retreated to their strongholds, and Forrest's command returned to picket duty, operating out of Spring Hill. For nearly six weeks, with a semi-independent command, Forrest fought small engagements with Union forces. He commanded a division with a brigade led by Brig. Gen. Frank C. Armstrong. On March 25 at Brentwood, Forrest surprised the Union garrison, maneuvered to cut off their retreat, and forced them to surrender. The 521 men he captured, ironically, had escaped during the battle at Thompson's Station.[16]

Sending his prisoners off with General Armstrong, Forrest dashed toward the Harpeth Railroad Bridge, a mile and a half from Brentwood. He encountered a stockade defended by 230 Union soldiers. Forrest demanded the surrender of the garrison, but they refused. Forrest brought up his artillery, sent a shot into the defenses causing the Union commander to reconsider and surrender his post. Forrest again captured men who had escaped at Thompson's Station.[17]

The victory at Brentwood was tainted a few days later when Forrest and Van Dorn had a disagreement and nearly fought. Both men had similar personalities and were spirited, and it did not take much to create friction. There are several versions of the story, but it seems that both men disagreed about how the Union property captured by Forrest should have been handled. Forrest's men kept the best weapons and mounts and turned into the

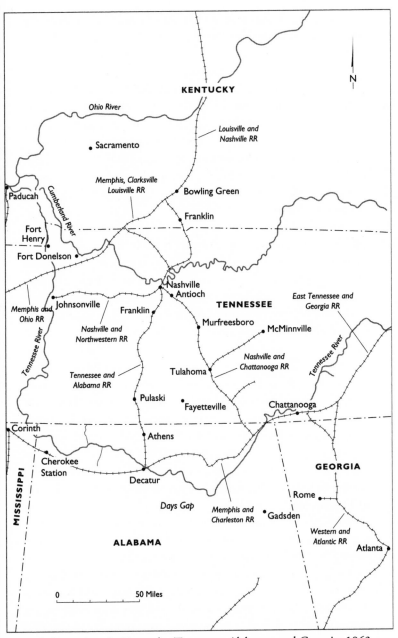

Forrest's Operations in Kentucky, Tennessee, Alabama, and Georgia, 1863.
Bill Nelson

Confederate quartermaster the rest. After a heated discussion, the disagreement ended with Forrest saying, "General Van Dorn, I think there are Yankees enough for you and me to fight without our fighting each other." They parted as friends, seeing each other for the last time before Van Dorn was killed a month later.[18]

In April Van Dorn and Forrest operated separately against the Union garrison in Franklin. During one of the reconnaissance missions, Union Maj. Gen. David S. Stanley, commanding the cavalry of the Department of the Cumberland, rode from Murfreesboro and on April 10 surprised Forrest on his flank. Couriers rode to Forrest, exclaiming that, "General Stanley has cut in behind you, has attacked Starnes' brigade, has captured the rear-guard battery, and is right in Armstrong's rear." Forrest, cool under fire, shouted so everyone could hear, "You say he is in Armstrong's rear, do you? Damn him! That's just where I have been trying to get him all day, and I'll be in his rear directly. Face your line of battle about! Armstrong, push your skirmishers forward—crowd 'em both ways!" Forrest managed to recapture the battery and the prisoners and drove the Union forces from the field.[19]

Since the Battle of Murfreesboro, the Union forces had remained content in their strongholds. In the spring of 1863, however, Maj. Gen. William S. Rosecrans decided to push Bragg and the Confederate Army of the Tennessee south of the Tennessee River. If Rosecrans could destroy Bragg's major supply lines to Chattanooga, the Confederates would have to retreat into Georgia. One of the two attempts to destroy the Confederate logistical arteries, especially the Western and Atlantic Railroad, was made by Col. Abel D. Streight. With a select command of two thousand men mounted on mules, which were thought to be appropriate for the area's rough terrain, Streight was to move through territory inhabited by Unionists.

Streight, however, encountered problems from the beginning. Many of his animals arrived in poor condition, and some were nearly dead. On the night of April 19, Confederates under the command of Col. Philip D. Roddey broke into Streight's corral and stampeded his animals. It took two days to recover about half of them and delayed the proposed raid.[20]

On April 21, Streight and Brig. Gen. Grenville M. Dodge with 5,500 men left Eastport, Mississippi, and arrived at Tuscumbia, Alabama, three days later. Dodge went along to attack Tuscumbia, to confuse the Confederates, and to allow Streight to get a head start. Streight took with him only 1,500 of his best men. Meanwhile, on the 23rd, Forrest received orders from Bragg to move quickly to join Colonel Roddey's 1,200 men and check the Union advance. Forrest rapidly moved part of his command to the relief of Roddey and brought the remainder up as fast as possible. While Forrest energetically engaged Dodge's troops, Streight slipped away to the south and began his eastward movement across Alabama. Forrest did not learn this until April 28, when Streight's "mule brigade" was on its way to Moulton, Alabama, more than thirty miles from Tuscumbia.[21]

Forrest ordered Roddey to watch and harass the retreating Federals under Dodge in order to keep the Union forces from reuniting. After learning that Streight's force had continued eastward, he realized that this was a planned raid. Forrest now personally supervised the necessary preparations to catch up with Streight. He doubled the teams of horses that would pull the artillery, inspected the men, and supervised the details of ammunition and food. At 1 A.M. on the morning of the 29th, he and his men began their pursuit.[22]

Streight had nearly a thirty-mile head start and left Moulton at midnight the 28th. Forrest and his men rode without a halt for seven hours, stopped to feed and rest the horses, and then pushed on, reaching Moulton before noon the next day. Streight had made seventeen miles to Day's Gap at Sand Mountain and camped for the night.[23]

On the 29th, Forrest continued his pursuit and arrived to within four miles of Day's Gap just after midnight. Streight, however, was still several hours ahead. Forrest's troops by now were exhausted, and he allowed them to rest. He sent his brother Capt. William Forrest and his famous Forty Scouts to continue the pursuit. They rode hard and passed between Streight's rear guard and his main force and in moonlight captured the unsuspecting Union solders guarding the rear of the column.[24]

William continued his advance until he could see the Union campfires and then rested his men. The Confederates were awakened before daylight the next morning by the enemy's braying mules. Streight, unaware that the enemy was so near, moved slowly up the mountain road. With Streight's column stretched along the road, Captain Forrest attacked. Bedford, meanwhile, also moved before daylight and divided his men, hoping to cut off Streight and be in a position to flank him.[25]

Streight now knew he would have to stand and fight. About two miles from the top of Sand Mountain, he laid a trap. He sent his mules and horses ahead and, hiding his men in the brush, waited for Bedford's brother. Following closely on the heels of the rear guard, William Forrest maintained his pressure and, as the last of his stragglers passed, Streight's men, on either side of the road, fired a volley into the Southern troops and emptied many saddles. A bullet struck William Forrest in the thigh and seriously wounded him.[26]

Bedford, now at the front, rushed to support William. During the initial charge by Forrest's men, Streight launched a counterattack. Forrest realized he had to stop Streight and ordered as many men into the line as possible. Normally some men remained behind to hold the horses. But all were instructed to tie their animals to the bough of a tree and advance. One of the men questioned what would happen if the charge failed and their horses were captured. Forrest remarked, "If we are whipped, we'll not need any horses."[27]

The countercharge by Streight, however, cost the Confederates two field pieces. The guns had been deployed so close to the enemy that when the horses that pulled them were killed, the gunners could not move them quickly enough to escape. Infuriated at this loss, Forrest tried to rally his men to retake the guns. Before he could get them formed, however, Streight had already disappeared along with the guns.[28]

Forrest rode among his men, saber drawn, trying to rally them to recover the guns. Streight, though, quickly moved six miles away before halting again. He was now on a ridge called Hog Mountain. Forrest pressed on both flanks of his enemy, but darkness made the advance ineffective. The major fighting ended at 10:00, when Streight withdrew again, leaving the two captured but spiked guns, as well as thirty wagons and teams scattered through the woods. During the day's pursuit, Forrest had had three more horses shot from beneath him, but he did not intend to let the Union troops rest. He reportedly said, "Whenever you see anything blue, shoot at it, and do all you can to keep up the scare." Streight fought two more actions that night trying to keep the Confederates from approaching too close.[29]

Forrest had successfully harassed the Federal column by using one portion of his command at a time, keeping the rest fresh. Streight realized his men could not keep this pace and hoped to find a defensible position where he could feed his horses and require Forrest to forage and lose time. At about 10:00 A.M. on May 1, Streight reached Blountsville, a little more than forty miles from Day's Gap. There he found corn to feed his animals, but he did not halt for long, continuing toward Gadsden.[30]

West of Blountsville, Forrest's men also fed their animals, and after two hours' sleep, they were off again in pursuit. In the past forty-eight hours they had ridden for all but four hours. Streight's rear guard was attacked before he could get his column out of Blountsville. Forrest managed to keep close to his enemy because of the reliable scouts of his brother William.[31]

One of these scouts, however, learned firsthand of Bedford Forrest's temper, his high expectations of thoroughness and reliability. Near Blountsville a scout rode up to Forrest, proclaiming excitedly that a force of Union cavalry was moving on a road parallel to the Confederates. The general said, "Did you see the Yankees?" The scout replied, "No; I did not see them myself, but . . . a citizen came galloping up on horseback and told me he had seen them." Forrest knew the scout was lying and in his "hands on" style of dealing with problems grabbed the man by the throat, dragged him from his horse, and placed him against a tree. After banging the scout's head on the tree for several moments, Forrest stopped and said, "Now, damn you, if you ever come to me again with a pack of lies, you won't get off so easily."[32]

Streight, meanwhile, reached the Black Warrior River, ten miles from Blountsville, and threw out a heavy line of skirmishers for protection as he got his men and animals over the river. After getting his artillery across, he was able to protect his skirmishers from the banks on the other side. During this time, Forrest halted his men for about three hours of rest and then crossed the river.[33]

Forrest's command was worn out. For three days, his men had been in the saddle, and some were now showing signs of exhaustion—literally falling asleep on their horses. Forrest knew that this was a critical point, so he addressed his men to encourage them and called on all to follow him. The entire command, now aroused from their weariness, cheered, remounted, and rode in pursuit of the Union column. It was not long before they overtook the Union troopers. Forrest now called for fifty of his best mounted men to attack the Union rear. This small force arrived, however, just as the Union troops torched a bridge, leaving them on one side of Black Creek with Streight's artillery on the other side.[34]

While reflecting on this predicament, Forrest rode to a farm near the bridge and asked how he could get across the creek. A tall attractive girl of about sixteen, named Emma Sansom, told the general that with a horse she could show them a hidden ford where his men could cross. With no time to lose, Forrest pulled Emma up to sit behind him. She guided him to a spot a half mile from the burned bridge. The Confederates drove off a small Federal detachment, quickly crossed, and were again on the Union heels.[35]

On May 2, Streight reached Gadsden, Alabama, being chased and harassed by Forrest's men. At every mile men and animals dropped from the Union column. Streight stopped in Gadsden to collect fresh mounts, allowing Forrest to close the distance. Streight's only hope now was to get to Rome, Georgia, cross the bridge over the Oostanaula River, and burn the bridge before Forrest could arrive. This would probably delay the Confederates two days and allow him to rest his troops, collect new mounts, and escape.[36]

On May 3, Forrest's men caught up with the Federal cavalry as they ate breakfast near the Alabama-Georgia state line, about twenty-five miles west of Rome. Some of the Union troops were so exhausted that they fell asleep during the skirmish fire. Driven from their camp, the Union troops rallied on a ridge. Forrest had about 600 men and might have rushed upon his enemy of about 1,400 men with an all-out charge. Instead, he decided to use a bluff on Colonel Streight.[37]

Forrest sent a flag of truce forward with the demand for immediate surrender. Streight asked to speak with Forrest personally, and they met in the woods. Streight would not surrender without knowing whether a force at least equal to his faced him. Forrest, however, said he would not "humiliate" his men in this way. At this moment, a section of Confederate artillery passed within view of the Union colonel, and he asked that no further troops be deployed forward. Forrest agreed and, when passing this word, asked his aide that the artillery section be kept moving in circles to make it appear that he had more artillery arriving.[38]

Streight, looking over Forrest's shoulders, saw the artillery pass again and again while the rebel troops marched in sight. Finally, he said, "Name of God! How many guns have you got? There's fifteen I've counted already!" Forrest replied, "I reckon that's all that has kept up." Streight still insisted he would not surrender. Forrest, now impatient, said, "I've got enough to whip you out of your boots" and shouted to his bugler, "Sound to mount." Streight then cried out, "I'll surrender."[39]

Forrest captured a total of 1,466 men here and bagged another 200 that had marched to secure the bridge at Rome. When Streight saw that Forrest's troops only numbered about one-third of his, he demanded his arms back so he could fight again.

Forrest just laughed at him and said, "Ah, Colonel, all is fair in love and war, you know."[40]

During the pursuit, Forrest's men averaged forty-one miles a day and captured a Union force of overwhelming number. Forrest had prevented the widespread destruction of Confederate infrastructure and industry and protected Bragg's supply lines. This brilliant accomplishment was not lost on the press, which recounted this feat for a month.[41]

After this remarkable achievement, General Bragg gave Forrest command of all the cavalry on the left flank of his army, a position vacated by the death of Van Dorn. With two brigades, Forrest served on picket duty, and for two weeks little occurred other than small skirmishes between Spring Hill and Columbia. Yet Forrest was to become embroiled in another argument and would receive his second war wound, one that nearly cost him his life.

The seeds of this misunderstanding originated at the Battle of Sand Mountain when the Union forces had captured Forrest's two guns. Despite the fact that he later recaptured them, Forrest had never been satisfied with the way his men had handled the field pieces. After reorganizing his forces in a larger command, he transferred the young lieutenant in charge of the guns lost at Sand Mountain. Lt. Andrew Wills Gould had left the guns on the field after many of the horses were killed or had become entangled with their gear. While Forrest never made a charge against Gould, the lieutenant felt the transfer was a reflection on his honor and sought to speak with Forrest.[42]

On the afternoon of June 13, 1863, Gould met Forrest at his headquarters in the Masonic building in Columbia. They began to discuss Gould's transfer in the hall. The meeting quickly became an argument as Gould, now excited, raised his voice. Witnesses claim that during the discussion Forrest had his left hand in his pocket and the other twirling a penknife. Gould had his hand on a pistol concealed by a duster. After a few moments of heated discussion, Forrest, not willing to change his order, walked away. Gould, unsatisfied with the answer, fired at Forrest, striking him near the hip. Forrest immediately grabbed Gould with one hand and with the other pulled open the blade of his knife with his teeth. Forrest struck Gould in the chest with the knife. Severely wounded, Gould broke away from Forrest's grasp and ran out the door into the street.[43]

Forrest also passed into the street and into the office of a doctor a few doors down. After a quick examination, the physician told Forrest that he needed immediate attention for this critical wound. Forrest exclaimed, "No damned man shall kill me and live!" Forrest ran out the door, snatched a pistol from the holster of a saddled horse, found a second gun, and began searching for Gould with a weapon in each hand.[44]

Gould, meanwhile, had run into a tailor shop and was lying on the counter, blood gushing from his wound. Upon hearing that Forrest was coming, he ran to the back door; Forrest fired and just missed. Gould, in his haste to escape, stumbled out the back door and fell to the ground. Forrest followed, and when he reached Gould believed his shot had struck the lieutenant and mortally wounded him. The general, in great pain, left him lying on the ground and was carried to a house for treatment. After Forrest underwent a careful examination, it was discovered that the pistol ball had struck no vital organ and he would probably live.[45]

Gould succumbed several days later, but not before reportedly calling for Forrest. The young lieutenant asked to see the general who was still too weak to get up from his bed and had to be carried to the hotel where Gould lay. Gould took Forrest by the hand and said, "General, I shall not be here long, and I was not willing to go away without seeing you in person." He continued, "How thankful I am that I am the one who is to die and that you are spared to the country." He concluded by saying, "What I did I did in a moment of rashness, and I want your forgiveness." Forrest leaned over the bed, forgave him, and spoke of his regret that the wound was fatal.[46]

Chapter 4

"I Cannot Be Responsible for the Fate of Your Command"

B Y JUNE 1863, General Rosecrans was prepared to push General Bragg and the Army of Tennessee out of middle Tennessee. Forrest had recuperated quickly enough to join his forces as they fell back toward Tullahoma, en route to Chattanooga. Forrest's men performed screening and rear guard duties for the army, and once Bragg settled in Chattanooga, Forrest was placed on the army's right flank. Bedford established his headquarters at Kingston, Tennessee, on the Tennessee River, forty-five miles southwest of Knoxville. The prospect of outpost duty did not appeal to Forrest, and he proposed to take four hundred men to "harass and destroy" boats on the Mississippi River. His request was denied on the grounds that he was too valuable for the army.[1]

On September 4, while Forrest chafed under Bragg's command, Rosecrans moved across the Tennessee River. The following day Knoxville was occupied without a shot being fired. The flanking moves by the Union army now threatened the Western and Atlantic Railroad, and Bragg was forced to evacuate Chattanooga. Rosecrans's eastward flanking movement, however, left his command strung out from Chattanooga to north Georgia. After realizing the Union predicament, Bragg began concentrating his forces. Maj. Gen. Simon Buckner's 8,000 men joined Bragg, and another 11,000 arrived from Mississippi. Jefferson Davis also sent Lt. Gen. James Longstreet and six brigades by train from Virginia.[2]

Bragg hoped to strike Rosecrans's columns as they emerged from the mountains. Bragg, long noted for snatching defeat from the jaws of victory, mismanaged his army by issuing complex orders and by allowing his subordinates to dawdle. This precipitated squabbling among the general officers, and the best opportunity to crush the Union army was lost.

Forrest, on the right, knew the enemy's predicament and tried to strike the exposed Union forces. But he had too few men to be more than an annoyance. During a fight at Tunnel Hill, Forrest received another bullet wound, near his spine. This wound, however, was less serious then his earlier wound, and he remained in the saddle.[3]

With more than 66,000 men under his command or nearby, Bragg began to move north to cross Chickamauga Creek with hopes of smashing Rosecrans's left and reoccupying Chattanooga. On September 18 the attack got under way and Longstreet's men began to arrive that afternoon. The opposing armies shifted troops, and by the 19th Rosecrans had moved northward closer to his supply lines and Bragg had moved southward.

While reconnoitering on the morning of the 19th, Forrest found that instead of the cavalry force that he faced the day before, Union infantry was massed at his front and overlapping his flank. Forrest immediately dismounted his men, told them to hold the Union advance, and sought help. Forrest eventually got support from four brigades, the last under the command of Brig. Gen. Matthew D. Ector. The fighting was intense, and Forrest rode up and down the line encouraging his men. In full sight of the enemy, he lost another horse. During the battle, General

Ector became concerned about his right flank and sent one of his aides to Forrest. Forrest told the aide, "Tell General Ector that he need not bother about his right flank; I'll take care of it." An hour later the aide returned with a message relating Ector's concerns for his left flank. This time Forrest became furious and shouted above the din of battle, "Tell General Ector that, by God, I am here, and will take care of his left flank as well as his right."[4]

At 1:30 Cheatham and five brigades relieved Forrest. The vicious daylong battle, along a four-mile front of dense woods and scattered clearings, ended with no victor but with the Union left bloodied. Bragg decided to attack the left again early the following day. Rosecrans, however, strengthened the position during the night.

The Confederates failed to attack until after 9:30 the next morning, losing the initiative. Forrest's men were dismounted and fought for two hours as infantry on the right. At 11:00 Rosecrans was misinformed that a gap had appeared in his line. He moved a division from his right to plug the hole and instead created a new gap. General Longstreet's men quickly discovered the breach in the Union line and began pouring through. The Union center collapsed, and much of the Federal army began to race toward Chattanooga.

Bragg now had an opportunity to annihilate the remnants of the Union army. Acting decisively, Union Major General George H. Thomas rallied the remaining men into a defensive stance and withstood the Confederate attacks until dusk and with composure withdrew. The Confederates had driven the Union forces from the field at Chickamauga in one of the war's bloodiest battles. Yet Bragg might have thoroughly defeated his enemy.

Forrest's force was exhausted, but his nature was to pursue his enemy. He set off with four hundred men to attack the Union rear. Forrest learned that the enemy was strung out along a long route and was trying to escape across the Tennessee River over a couple of pontoons. He sent a note back to Lt. Gen. Leonidas Polk that the Union forces "are evacuating as hard as they can go . . . we ought to press forward as rapidly as possible." During an

attack on the Union rear, Forrest lost another horse while leading a charge. The animal was struck in the neck, and with blood
spurting out, Forrest realized that it would bleed to death before
he reached his destination. Always one to improvise, he leaned
forward, while at full gallop, and plugged the wound with his
finger. The horse lived to deliver Forrest and died shortly after
the general dismounted.[5]

Bragg, however, would not press the retreating Federal forces.
Forrest, seeing the enemy slip away and knowing that Bragg had
an opportunity to punish his enemy, became impatient. He rode
to Bragg's headquarters to plead in person with him. Unable to
convince his superior, Forrest rode back to his men muttering,
"What does he fight battles for?"[6]

On September 28, Bragg wrote a dispatch to Forrest ordering
him to turn over the troops in his command. Forrest became en-
raged and dictated a letter to Bragg accusing him of duplicity
and lying. He also stated that he would pay Bragg a visit to discuss the issue in person.[7]

Forrest kept his promise. He arrived at Bragg's tent and, already fuming, passed by the sentry without returning the salute.
Bragg, in the tent alone, stood up to greet Forrest and offered his
hand. Forrest stood stiffly and said icily, "I am not here to pass ci-
vilities or compliments with you . . . You commenced your cow-
ardly and contemptible persecution of me soon after the battle of
Shiloh . . . You did it because I reported to Richmond facts while
you reported damned lies." Forrest continued his tirade as Bragg
stepped back toward the corner of the tent. "You robbed me of
my command in Kentucky, and gave it to one of your favorites."
Forrest then alleged that Bragg had, in the spirit of revenge and
spite, driven him into west Tennessee during the winter of 1862
with improper arms and insufficient ammunition trying to "ruin"
him and his career. After returning from this mission well
equipped, Forrest charged that Bragg had again begun "his work
of spite and persecution." He believed that Bragg had tried to
humiliate him by transferring to another unit a brigade that earlier "won a reputation for successful fighting. . . ." Forrest contin-

ued his tirade, and Bragg now sat in his chair. "I have stood your meanness as long as I intend to. You have played the part of a damned scoundrel, and are a coward, and if you were any part of a man I would slap your jaws and force you to resent it." Forrest concluded, "You may as well not issue any more orders to me, for I will not obey them . . . [and] if you ever again try to interfere with me or cross my path it will be at the peril of your life."[8]

Forrest stormed from the tent, leaving Bragg dumbfounded and those who heard the exchange astonished. One officer spoke to Forrest, "Well, you are in for it now." But Forrest knew Bragg and replied, "He'll never say a word about it, he'll be the last man to mention it; and marking my word, he'll take no action in the matter. I will ask to be relieved and transferred to a different field, and he will not oppose it." Forrest had defended his honor. Earlier in his life, he might have used violence. His behavior clearly showed that he believed Bragg was not his equal.[9]

Bragg transferred Forrest to Wheeler's command. Knowing that he could not work under Wheeler, Forrest resigned his commission. After a meeting with President Davis in Montgomery, Forrest was placed in a semi-independent position in northern Mississippi. He would report to Maj. Gen. Stephen D. Lee, who commanded all the cavalry in Mississippi. Forrest, however, took only about three hundred men with him. His new headquarters was in Okolona, Mississippi.

Forrest once again had to create a command. Getting new recruits from the Union-occupied areas of western Tennessee and Kentucky, however, would be difficult. By the end of November, though, he had about 450 riders and planned to make a raid into western Tennessee to recruit and secure supplies for his poorly mounted and equipped men.[10]

On December 1, Forrest led a small column north toward the Memphis and Charleston Railroad. With so few mounts, he could take only two pieces of artillery. Forrest was able to advance nearly thirty-five miles before running into Union forces outside Bolivar, Tennessee. By December 6, he was in Jackson, where he established a headquarters and began to recruit. He recruited between fifty and a hundred men a day. Without any government funds, he had to use $120,000 of his own money to continue.[11]

Forrest's growing presence worried the Union leaders, and they began to march against him. Forrest, whose scouts were placed well in the field, soon reported these movements. Five brigadier generals began concentrating against Forrest: Andrew J. Smith left Columbus, Kentucky; William Sooy Smith started from middle Tennessee; George Crook departed Huntsville, Alabama; Joseph A. Mower left Corinth; and Benjamin Grierson marched from LaGrange, Tennessee.[12]

Forrest, anticipating the need to escape rapidly, had his men sink the ferry at Bolivar to be raised later. He also sent a flying column ahead to search for a crossing at Estenaula over the Hatchie River. Forrest divided his 3,600 men into three large detachments; the largest of these included many of his 3,000 new recruits, most of them still unarmed. By December 23 his men were riding southward.[13]

Forrest knew he had to delay his pursuers and on the night of the 24th sent forward his personal escort, comprising about sixty men. They chased the enemy picket guard back toward the main camp and moved into a cornfield that bordered the Union camp. In order to deceive their foe, Forrest's men formed into a long line ten paces apart. Each man, in a voice as loud as possible, began shouting orders as if he were commanding a company. Seeing the Union camp now in disorder, the lieutenant in charge of the escort shouted, "Forward, brigade; charge!" The Federal forces, thinking they were under attack by a much larger unit, broke camp and moved ten miles farther away.[14]

Forrest's main force had to contend with swollen rivers and swampy bottomland to escape the converging Union columns. Hindering his movement were the two hundred beef cattle and three hundred hogs accompanying his wagon train. On Christmas Day, the ferryboat on the Hatchie River at Estenaula capsized, dumping the horses and the teamsters into the icy water. Without hesitation, Forrest dove into the water up to his armpits and cut the struggling horses out of their harnesses to save them. During this rather unusual action, a recent conscript began loudly proclaiming that he had no intention of going into the water. Most of Forrest's men knew better than to complain, especially in his presence, but the conscript continued loudly proclaiming that "he wasn't goin' to get down in that water, no sir, not for nobody." Forrest climbed up the muddy bank, strode over to the man, and without a word picked him up by his collar and his pants and threw him into the water.[15]

By midday Forrest had his men across the Hatchie River. But the Union forces were still at his heels. On the 26th, his pursuers caught up again, and in another bluff he ordered his armed and unarmed men into battle, hoping that the great numbers would discourage the Union force. A sharp fight ensued, and the Confederates drove the Federal cavalry away, eluding for good all the Union pursuers. Forrest's second raid into west Tennessee, with six hundred armed men, gained him three thousand recruits while he eluded some twenty thousand Union troops.[16]

During the raid, Forrest was promoted to major general and now reported to the new head of the department, Leonidas Polk. Polk created a new Northern Cavalry Department with Forrest in command. It embraced west Tennessee and northern Mississippi. Forrest organized his men into four brigades, two of these forming a division under Brig. Gen. James R. Chalmers.[17]

Also while Forrest rode through Tennessee, Union Major General William T. Sherman had finalized plans for a major campaign. He proposed marching from Vicksburg, Mississippi, eastward to capture Meridian, Mississippi. The capture of this major railroad center would cripple Confederate rail traffic both north and south and east and west. Control of the area between Meridian and the Mississippi River would also cripple Rebel communications and deny a large area to the Confederacy for supplies and recruits.

On February 10, Sherman ordered Brig. Gen. William Sooy Smith and seven thousand cavalry and thirty pieces of artillery from Memphis to raid southward down the Mobile and Ohio

Railroad. He would meet with Smith in Meridian with two columns totaling twenty thousand men. On the 14th, Sherman arrived at Meridian, after a few skirmishes, and waited six days for Smith, who never arrived. With no word from Smith, he had to return to Vicksburg having accomplished a small portion of his goals.

Smith did not even begin his journey until the day after he was to be in Meridian. Forrest had only about 2,500 men, mostly new recruits, some of whom were not yet armed. He realized he could not fight on par with this overwhelming Union force and closely watched his enemy, looking for an opening, probing and skirmishing with Smith's column as it advanced.[18]

On February 20, during a skirmish at the Sakatonchee River, Forrest rode to the front and met with Chalmers. Forrest's face was "greatly flushed," and Chalmers noticed that Forrest was more excited than usual. When Forrest asked about the situation at the front, Chalmers could not give him any details, and both rode to observe the skirmish. Passing through a steady fire with bullets passing dangerously close, Forrest noticed a rebel soldier "coming at full tilt" toward him. Dismounted and hatless, the man had thrown away his gun and equipment in order to get to the rear quickly. Forrest dismounted, rushed to the soldier, grabbed him by the collar, and dragged him to the roadside. Picking up a piece of brush, Forrest gave the man "one of the worst thrashings" Chalmers had ever seen. Forrest then turned the terrified soldier loose and roared, "Now—damn you, go back to the front and fight: you might as well be killed there as here, for if you ever run away again you will not get off so easy."[19]

The next day Forrest realized that Smith's movement at the river was a feint designed to allow him to retreat. The Union force began to move to West Point, but Forrest was "unwilling they should leave the county without a fight." Forrest pursued Sooy Smith like he had Streight, harrying his rear guard relentlessly.[20]

Forrest led the chase with his escort and drove the Union column northward. During a skirmish at West Point on the 21st,

Forrest again directed the assault. One of his men wrote, "his immediate presence seemed to inspire every one with his terrible energy, which was more like that of a piece of powerful steam machinery than of a human being."[21]

The following day the Union forces arrived at Okolona and formed into a defensive line. Forrest decided to use his usual tactic of showing a frontal attack while probing the flanks. This succeeded, and Smith's line broke in confusion. Utterly "disorganized," Smith lost five pieces of artillery in a running fight. The Union forces re-formed in a defensive stand on a ridge several miles down the road, where Forrest's youngest brother Jeffrey was mortally wounded in a charge. Bedford rushed to his brother and held him as he died. Emotionally crushed by the loss of his brother, Forrest immediately rode to the front to exact vengeance. One of his staff officers called for the surgeon, "Doctor, hurry after the general; I am afraid he will be killed!" Forrest met the enemy and fought in a hand-to-hand fight with his escort at his side. Col. Robert McCulloch, one of his brigade commanders, realized the peril and shouted, "My God, men, will you see them kill your general? I will go to his rescue if not a man follows me!"[22] McCulloch and his men rushed into the fray while Forrest dispatched three Union cavalrymen. In the confusion and carnage, Forrest lost another horse, mounted a second horse, and rode only about 150 yards before this mount was also killed.[23]

Smith hoped to escape with his supply train and stopped to check Forrest once more before sunset. At this point, Forrest's men were scattered, tired, and low on ammunition. The Confederates found the Union forces drawn up in three lines across a large field. Forrest withdrew his men behind a gully and awaited the Federal horsemen. With bugles sounding the charge, the Union cavalry rode to within sixty yards of the Confederate lines. The Union troopers met a murderous volley, which sent them reeling rearward and left a large number of dead and wounded on the field. A second charge was thrown back at forty yards. During a third charge, the Confederates allowed the

Union soldiers to ride within twenty yards before unleashing a volley. The Union cavalrymen reached the gully, but the Confederates were able to repulse the Union soldiers with their revolvers.[24]

After three days of fighting, the Union forces were demoralized, fully broken, and on their way to Memphis. Forrest had lost 27 killed, 97 wounded, and 20 missing. Smith lost 54 killed, 179 wounded, and 155 missing.[25]

Forrest's actions in the Meridian Campaign are no less than amazing. The Confederate forces were nearly one-third the size of Sooy Smith's. They were newly organized and poorly armed. They met and pursued, for more than fifty miles, some of the Union's best cavalry units supported by twenty pieces of artillery. As during the Streight raid, Forrest never relented. Despite the exhaustion of his troops, he continually harassed the Federal column and never allowed it to rest. This allowed Forrest to strike from many sides and gave the impression that he had superior numbers.

Forrest single-handedly checked the Union's plans in Mississippi. Sherman was chagrined and disappointed at Smith's performance. Ulysses S. Grant was impressed with his Confederate adversary. He called Forrest an "able" leader and said the outcome of battles are often "due to the way troops are officered, and for the particular kind of warfare which Forrest carried on, neither army could present a more effective officer than he was."[26]

After the Sooy Smith "stampede," Forrest rode to Polk's headquarters at Demopolis, Alabama. Polk discussed with Forrest plans for another raid into Tennessee and Kentucky for mounts and supplies and the control of western Tennessee. To help accomplish these goals, Polk attached fragments of three Kentucky regiments to Forrest's command. Brig. Gen. Abraham Buford, an 1841 graduate of West Point and a Mexican War veteran, also joined. Forrest reorganized his force into two divisions, one under Chalmers and the other under Buford, each with two brigades.

On March 15, Forrest moved out of camp with Buford's division and some men on foot. Five days later, they reached Jackson, Tennessee, after a march of about 140 miles. Forrest noted as he advanced that the Union forces and "roving bands of deserters and tories" had stripped the countryside and robbed the local populace. He pointed in particular to Col. Fielding Hurst and his regiment of "renegade Tennesseeans" who extorted money from the town of Jackson. Hurst also tortured and killed one of Forrest's lieutenants who was sent to Jackson to gather absentees and deserters. His murderers mutilated him, cut off his nose and his genitals, and skinned his face.[27] For Forrest, this opened a new vista for warfare in the backcountry. These new rules of engagement were not lost on Forrest or his men.

Marching northward to Trenton on the 22nd, Forrest set up a recruiting office. The following day he dispatched Col. William L. Duckworth and five hundred men to capture Union City, about thirty miles farther north. The Union forces were well entrenched, and after several charges Duckworth realized that, without artillery, he could not drive the Union forces from their earthworks. Using a ruse, he made his command appear larger than it was and sent in a note with Forrest's forged signature saying he would give no quarter if he had to storm the fort. The Union garrison surrendered, netting Duckworth and the Confederacy about five hundred prisoners, three hundred horses, arms, and stores.[28]

Forrest, meanwhile, rode north to Paducah, Kentucky. Arriving on the afternoon of 25 March, he immediately attacked Fort Anderson on the north side of town. After an hour of skirmishing, Forrest sent in a flag of truce demanding the surrender of the fort defended by more than 650 men and Union gunboats in the river. The note was almost identical to those Forrest had sent earlier to Union officers. It stated he had sufficient force to take the fort, he wanted to avoid bloodshed, and the troops would be treated as prisoners of war. The note concluded with the text "if I have to storm your works, you may expect no quarter."[29]

The Union commander knew he had a strong position and had no intention of surrendering his garrison. Forrest realized that an assault would necessarily sacrifice his men and decided to hold the Union force in the fort while he destroyed and captured the enemy's stores. Unfortunately, one of his brigade officers, without orders or support, tried to take the fort. Forrest lost more than two dozen men killed and wounded.[30]

Forrest then moved back to Jackson, Tennessee, having secured some much needed supplies. His losses were fifteen killed and forty-two wounded since moving on Paducah. According to his records, he had captured 612, killed 79, and wounded 102 Union soldiers. He was confident that he could control west Tennessee and decided to attack Fort Pillow, "as they have horses and supplies which we need."[31]

In 1861 the Confederates constructed Fort Pillow on the east bank of the Mississippi River forty miles north of Memphis. The Federal forces occupied the fort in May 1862, but did little to further strengthen it. The garrison depended on the Union gunboats for added security. The fort had three separate lines of entrenchments. The first began about six hundred yards from the river and stretched from Coal Creek for about two miles to the southwest. The Confederates built a shorter line inside this original work. The Union forces built a third and even smaller work about 125 yards long, enclosing only the high angular bluff at the edge of the river. The fort mounted six pieces of artillery on a parapet six to eight feet high and four to six feet thick. A ditch twelve feet wide and eight feet deep in front helped protect the works against an assault. Several rows of barracks and storehouses were on the south side of the fort. The Union gunboat *New Era* lay in the river as added protection.[32]

Maj. Lionel F. Booth commanded the fort. He had 277 men in a battalion of Tennessee Unionists (Tennessee Tories) led by Maj. William Bradford. Many of these men had escaped from Forrest's command. Also in the fort were another 305 men of the 6th U.S. Colored Heavy Artillery and the 2d U.S. Colored Light Artillery. Most of these men were former slaves.[33]

Before Forrest began his approach to the fort, he sent out several diversions to hold the nearby Union garrisons in place. On April 10 he gave Chalmers command of the main column until he arrived. In a steady drizzle, the brigades moved from their encampments and began to arrive before Fort Pillow at about 5:30 on the morning of April 12.[34]

The Confederates immediately invested the fort and by sunup had driven the Union skirmishers out of the outermost rifle pits. The second line of rifle pits were abandoned at 8, leaving the Union garrison defending only the inner fort. This allowed the Confederates to crawl among the stumps, logs, and underbrush to obtain good defensive positions, and the sharpshooters took the parapet under fire. This fire wounded and killed many of the fort's officers and took a toll on the African American artillerymen. Early in the fight, the sharpshooters killed Major Booth and his adjutant. Command of the fort fell on the shoulders of Major Bradford. The fort's artillery could not stop the Confederates from closing, and, though the gunboat *New Era* fired, it added nothing to the defense.[35]

Forrest arrived during the morning, having ridden more than seventy miles in just over twenty-four hours. Forrest immediately began to assess personally the defenses. As he advanced close to the fort, a bullet struck his horse; it reared, threw the general to the ground, and then fell on him. Badly bruised, Forrest mounted another animal. One of Forrest's adjutants begged him to reconnoiter on foot, but Forrest told him he was "just as apt to be hit one way as another." The general later had a second horse killed and another wounded before he satisfied himself with the deployment of the enemy and the terrain.[36]

Forrest made some adjustments to his lines after reconnoitering the defenses. He increased the number of sharpshooters from every position around the fort. He also saw that the fort had a blind spot on the left, created by the rows of barracks 150 yards from the works. The Federal troops had unsuccessfully tried to burn these buildings, but the Confederates occupied them before they could accomplish the task. This allowed the Confederates to silence the artillery on that side of the fort. With 1,500 men on the field, Forrest was now ready to talk.[37]

Forrest sent in a flag of truce and a message to Major Booth.

In part it read, "The conduct of the officers and men garrisoning Fort Pillow has been such as to entitle them to being treated as prisoners of war." The message further demanded the unconditional surrender of the garrison and again promised to treat the men as prisoners. He closed with the statement "Should my demand be refused, I cannot be responsible for the fate of your command."[38]

When the note was handed to the Union officers, there was discussion about whether the African Americans would also be treated as prisoners of war. Forrest and Chalmers both replied affirmatively. The message reached Major Bradford, who replied for Booth. He asked for one hour to consult with his staff and the officers on the gunboat.[39]

Forrest was now put in a difficult situation that altered the events of the battle and began the ensuing controversy. As the officers negotiated the truce, three steamers began ascending the river. The army transport *Olive Branch*, full of Union troops, was one of these. Forrest could not allow these vessels to support the fort, so he gave the Union officers twenty minutes to reach a decision and declined the surrender of the *New Era*. If he received no response after twenty minutes, he would "assault the works."[40]

During this time, however, the fort never hoisted signals to relay that a truce was being discussed in order to stop the advance of the steamers. With the army transport crowding steam to get up the river, Forrest had to negate this advantage. He sent four hundred men to the riverbank to keep enemy troops from landing. These men were instructed to take no part in the assault but were to prevent the escape of the garrison by water and to "fight everything *blue* between wind and water until yonder flag comes down." Forrest was later blamed for violating the truce. These men, though, did not take part in the assault. As it was, however, these men would later become a fateful part of the battle.[41]

Forrest was now becoming anxious. As the second note went back to the Union commander, a question arose as to whether Forrest was actually on the field. Intensifying the atmosphere were the taunts made by the men inside the fort. They openly defied the Confederates and suggested they "come and take the fort." Forrest, amid the banter between the two sides, rode within view of the fort in hopes that his presence would induce the Union leaders to capitulate. In an effort to stall the Confederate assault, Union leaders sent Forrest another note written in pencil on a scrap of soiled paper. It read, "Your demand does not produce the desired effect." Forrest sent it back stating he must have an answer yes or no. Again, another note was brought forward. "General: I will not surrender."[42]

The flags of truce were withdrawn, and Forrest ordered his men ready to make the assault. Forrest's men were directed not to fire a shot until they were inside the fort. The sharpshooters were instructed to keep the Union garrison below the parapets so that the Confederates could cross the ditch and climb into the fort without severe losses.[43]

At about 4, the bugler sounded the charge and more than a thousand men in front of the fort sprang to their feet. The rebel yell filled the air as they moved quickly to cross the ground in front of the parapets. The fort's defenders discharged the guns harmlessly over the rebels' heads, and Forrest's men reached the fort virtually unharmed. Forming human scaling ladders, they quickly got over the earthworks. The Confederates now began emptying their guns into the soldiers on the firing steps. Panic ensued, and the Union forces broke and ran.[44]

The first to break for the rear were the white Tennesseans. This left the black artillery units to bear the brunt of the assault until they too fled. Unfortunately, now they were between Forrest's men and the Tennessee Tories, and they took early heavy casualties. The Confederates entered the fort so quickly that the garrison failed to cut down the American flag. With so many of the fort's officers killed earlier by the sharpshooters, the men inside became a mob. Some begged for surrender, others feigned death, and still others continued the fight.[45]

The Union soldiers fled to the river under a prearranged plan, all the while being fired upon by the Confederates. The plan called for the Union troops to get to the river and drop under the

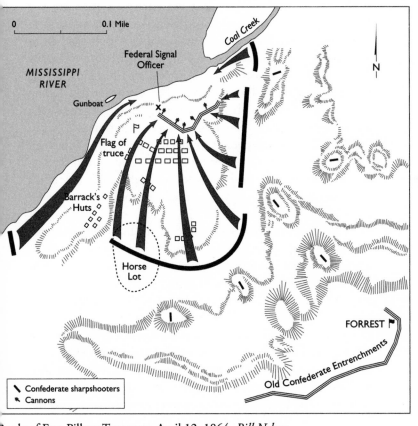

0   0.1 Mile

Coal Creek

Federal Signal
Officer

MISSISSIPPI
RIVER

N

Gunboat

Flag of
truce

Barrack's
Huts

Horse
Lot

FORREST

Old Confederate Entrenchments

Confederate sharpshooters
Cannons

Battle of Fort Pillow, Tennessee, April 12, 1864. *Bill Nelson*

bank so that the *New Era* could decimate the charging Confederates with canister from its guns. The garrison had already brought cases of extra ammunition and guns to the spot so that they could carry on the fight until the gunboat drove the enemy away.[46]

Major Bradford was heard to say, "Boys, save your lives." But as the Union soldiers arrived at the water, the *New Era* was steaming away up the river. The huddled Union troops, some still fighting, were now being slaughtered by the troops Forrest had sent to stop the landing of Union soldiers from the *Olive Branch*. They were perfectly positioned on the flank of the Union troops massed at the river. The Confederate flanking force had no idea the fight should be stopped until they saw the flag lowered. Scores of Union soldiers also died trying to escape in the river. The Confederates poured in a deadly fire on the men on the bank and in the water for several minutes until the flag was cut down. The entire battle, from the time the bugle sounded until the last shot was fired, was only about twenty minutes.[47]

This situation alone might have caused a furor, but the fighting had an even uglier side. The taunting by the Union garrison worked many of Forrest's Tennessee troops into a frenzy. When they attacked, they did so with extra zeal. As the men poured into the fort, there is ample evidence that there was additional slaughter, particularly of the African American soldiers, after they surrendered. This happened as the rebels streamed over the ramparts and all along the route as they chased the Union mob under the riverbank. How many were killed is unknown, and the debate began shortly after the smoke cleared.

Despite the fact that the colors were never lowered and the fort was never surrendered, Forrest clearly lost control of his men. He intended to capture the garrison without bloodshed. The casualty figures were about 40 percent, but for the African Americans, they were as high as 64 percent. The dynamics of the battle can, in part, account for this. The blacks suffered the full brunt of the initial Confederate assault; they retreated between the Confederate forces and the Union Tennessee Regiment and

Nathan Bedford Forrest prior to the Civil War. At nearly forty years of age, he had amassed a fortune and served as an alderman in Memphis. *Memphis Pink Palace Museum*

Nathan Bedford Forrest's younger brother, Capt. William Forrest, led the famous "Forty Scouts." He was said to be the only man Bedford feared. John Allen Wyeth, *Life of General Nathan Bedford Forrest* (New York: Harper & Bros., 1899)

Col. Jeffrey E. Forrest was killed at the Battle of Okolona in February 1864. Forrest held Jeffrey as he died and then rode into battle to exact vengeance. John Allen Wyeth, *Life of General Nathan Bedford Forrest* (New York: Harper & Bros., 1899)

Brig. Gen. James R. Chalmers commanded a division under Forrest and played a prominent role in the operations in northern Mississippi, Kentucky, and western Tennessee in 1864. John Allen Wyeth, *Life of General Nathan Bedford Forrest* (New York: Harper & Bros., 1899)

A disagreement between Maj. Gen. Earl Van Dorn and Forrest nearly ended in violence. *National Archives*

Maj. Gen. Joseph Wheeler commanded Forrest and his men at the Battle of Dover, Tennessee. After the defeat there, Forrest told Wheeler "I will be in my coffin before I will fight again under your command." *National Archives*

Brig. Gen. Abraham Buford commanded one of Forrest's divisions.
National Archives

Bedford Forrest usually urged his men into battle with the words "Forward, men, and mix with 'em." His inclination to lead his men in combat cost him four wounds and twenty-nine horses. John Allen Wyeth, *Life of General Nathan Bedford Forrest* (New York: Harper & Bros., 1899)

Without alerting the Union forces, Forrest and nearly seven hundred men escaped Fort Donelson in February 1862. John Allen Wyeth, *Life of General Nathan Bedford Forrest* (New York: Harper & Bros., 1899)

The commanding officer at Fort Pillow sends word to Forrest, refusing his plea for the garrison to surrender. The overwhelming Confederate force captured the fort about fifteen minutes after the attack began. John Allen Wyeth, *Life of General Nathan Bedford Forrest* (New York: Harper & Bros., 1899)

The Confederate attackers storm over the parapets at Fort Pillow with few casualties. Once in the fort, they quickly overwhelmed the Union garrison. In a controversy that persists today, the high number of casualties among the Union's African-American troops led to accusations that Forrest's men had perpetrated a racially motivated massacre. John Allen Wyeth, *Life of General Nathan Bedford Forrest* (New York: Harper & Bros., 1899)

Forrest in his lieutenant general's uniform. *Alabama Department of Archives and History*

Col. Abel D. Streight led a Union raid through northern Alabama. Forrest's pursuit and capture of this overwhelming Union force was a brilliant accomplishment. *Library of Congress*

During the Streight Raid, Emma Sansom bravely led Forrest to an alternative crossing at Black Creek that enabled the Confederates to continue their pursuit of the Union forces. John Allen Wyeth, *Life of General Nathan Bedford Forrest* (New York: Harper & Bros., 1899)

Col. Benjamin H. Grierson led the Union cavalry at the Battle of Brice's Cross Roads on June 10, 1864. There, Forrest defeated Grierson's force by noon and then defeated separately the Union infantry sent to reinforce Grierson. *Library of Congress*

At Brice's Cross Roads, Brig. Gen. Samuel Davis Sturgis suffered one of the Union's most embarrassing defeats at the hands of Forrest. *National Archives*

Maj. Gen. Andrew Jackson Smith had some
success against Forrest at Tupelo, Mississippi, in
July 1864. *Library of Congress*

Brig. Gen. James Harrison Wilson overwhelmed Forrest and his dwindling command at Selma, Alabama, in April 1865. Wilson was one of the few Union officers to defeat Forrest. *National Archives*

Nathan Bedford Forrest after the war. He claimed the war left him "wrecked . . . completely used up—shot all to pieces, crippled up . . . a beggar." Yet, he emerged from the war one of the most influential and popular men in western Tennessee. He, like many of his fellow Southerners, could not salvage the remains of his pre-war life. After the war he became the first leader of the Ku Klux Klan. *Library of Congress*

In 1905, Forrest and his wife were placed to rest beneath this statue in Memphis, Tennessee. *Library of Congress*

then died at and in the river. Racial antipathy only fueled the carnage. Blame for this ugly event in the Civil War falls squarely on Forrest's shoulders.

The Union had 308 survivors out of the garrison of 585. Forrest lost a mere 14 killed and 86 wounded. Confederate officers tried to open communication with the Union gunboats to take the wounded, but they fled instead. The Federal prisoners buried their dead, and the following day a Union transport took off the wounded.[48]

This controversy would become politicized. Republicans were looking for issues to weaken the Peace Democrats, and they formed a joint congressional committee headed by extreme radicals Senator Benjamin F. Wade and Representative Daniel W. Gooch. The committee called white and black witnesses to testify. With more than a hundred pages of testimony, the committee concluded that during the flag of truce Forrest's men "treacherously gained" the positions to assault the fort; they indiscriminately slaughtered the inhabitants without regard to age, sex, or race; and they committed other atrocities such as burning and burying men alive.[49]

Silence from the Confederate side only added to the implications of a massacre. Forrest, however, wrote his final report to General Polk on April 26. It was written before the congressional investigation, and he never mentioned any slaughter. It was not forwarded to Richmond because of Polk's death on June 14, during the Atlanta Campaign. No one in Richmond read it until August, and then was it published only to try to silence and refute the Northern claims of atrocities.[50]

Despite the fact that all the witnesses were hostile to the Confederates, there were enough inconsistencies and contradictions within the testimony to cast a pall over all the information gathered. Certainly Forrest could not be implicated personally in the crimes or the massacre. The burned bodies were those of dead Union soldiers left in the barracks and tents when the Union soldiers burned them. The burying of men alive was pure illusion, considering that the Union troops buried their own dead. There were no women or children in the fort; all had been removed before the fight. The vast majority of the African American casualties came in the action under the bluffs and in the water from the flanking column, not from a systemized slaughter in the fort after the flag was cut down.[51]

Forrest, however, as well as his men, was not without prejudice. Forrest had no misgivings about killing Union soldiers, white or black. In fact, while he had a paternalistic relationship with his own slaves, he saw African Americans as "deluded" and said that "Negro soldiers cannot cope with southerners." He stated that "I slaughter no man except in open warfare, and that my prisoners, both white and black, are turned over to my Government to be dealt with as it may direct."[52]

Major Bradford must also share the blame. He could have diffused the situation. Had he surrendered to Forrest's overwhelming force, it was promised that his men, both black and white, would be treated as prisoners of war. Bradford, who knew well the elements of his command, allowed his men to taunt the Confederates and delayed the surrender, hoping that the Union gunboats could come to his aid. This only increased the animosity between the two sides.

This battle will continue to create disagreement. It is clear that in the heat of the battle, Forrest's men killed a number of men as they tried to surrender. These deaths appeared to be isolated events, not a wholesale group effort. Had it been, there would have been no African American prisoners. While it was not premeditated, it still does not absolve Forrest and his men from blame. Simply, the Confederates entered the fort in an emotional frenzy brought on by the taunts of their enemies, many of them former slaves in uniform. Forrest lost control of his men, and he shoulders the responsibility for the unnecessary deaths.

Chapter 5

"Forrest Is the Very Devil"

FORREST AND HIS ESCORT rode from Fort Pillow on the night of April 12. Bedford traveled while still suffering from exhaustion and the fall he took before the attack. On the 13th, Forrest and his men arrived in Brownsville, Tennessee, to a hero's welcome. The following day they traveled to Jackson, reestablished his headquarters there, and immediately began to arrange for recruiting and gathering horses and supplies for his next operation.[1]

In Jackson the mail brought Forrest news of his youngest brother's death from pneumonia. Lt. Col. Aaron Forrest was the second of his brothers to die during the war. The mail that arrived also carried evidence of Bragg's continued animosity toward Forrest. Never one to observe faithfully the chain of command, Forrest had written President Davis about his latest operations and sent the president's wife a "beautiful flag" captured by his troops. Davis forwarded the report to Bragg for comment, who took this opportunity to criticize Forrest with an acid endorsement.[2]

Bedford, however, had little time for petty quarrels. Major

General Sherman was preparing to move nearly 100,000 men from Chattanooga to engage Gen. Joseph E. Johnston's 53,000-man Army of Tennessee near Dalton, Georgia. Sherman planned to strike at Atlanta, a crucial Confederate industrial supply and communication center, and at the same time Gen. Ulysses S. Grant would strike at Gen. Robert E. Lee's army guarding Richmond. Forrest had the capacity to threaten Sherman's lengthened communications in such a way that the whole campaign might be at risk. A single-track railroad from the Nashville and Chattanooga depots would supply his whole campaign.

Facing Forrest in the coming campaign was a new head of cavalry, Brig. Gen. Samuel D. Sturgis. A graduate of West Point, Sturgis had served in the Mexican War and fought with distinction in both the Eastern and Western theatres and was brevetted twice for gallant service. Sherman wrote, "I have sent Sturgis down to take command . . . and whip Forrest."[3]

Sherman sent Sturgis to strike at Forrest and to defeat him so that the Confederates could not harass his line of communications. On June 1 Sturgis began the trip from Memphis with more than 8,000 men, 22 pieces of artillery, and 250 wagons. He planned to strike the Mobile and Ohio Railroad at Corinth, then possibly move south as far as Macon or Columbus, Georgia, via Tupelo and Okolona, all the time hoping to draw Forrest into battle. More than one thousand of the five thousand infantry that accompanied the column were African Americans who had sworn to avenge the "massacre" at Fort Pillow.[4] The trip, however, did not begin well for Sturgis. Rain turned the roads into quagmires, and it took a week for his men to slog seventy miles southeast to Ripley, Mississippi.

On June 6 Forrest was still in Tupelo, Mississippi, having been recalled from a raid into Middle Tennessee. Pulling his widely scattered brigades together, Forrest began assembling his units at Booneville, twenty miles east of Sturgis's column. In an effort to slow Sturgis, Forrest began deploying skirmishers across Sturgis's route. Sturgis, however, continued southeast and by

June 9 had moved his column on a road toward Guntown, a station on the Mobile and Ohio Railroad. Forrest, still struggling to muster his dispersed forces, managed to have most of them together by the 9th. Delayed by muddy roads were his twelve pieces of artillery under his chief of artillery, Capt. John W. Morton. Forrest still planned to intercept Sturgis just south of his present position.[5]

Maj. Gen. Stephen D. Lee had directed Forrest to march to Okolona in hopes of luring the Union force farther south, where more Confederates could concentrate and attack. But Lee also gave Forrest discretion to attack the enemy. Forrest knew that despite the fact that he was greatly outnumbered, the road that the Union forces used was narrow and muddy. The dense woods, made up of blackjack and scrub oak, with only a few cleared fields, would also impede their progress. Forrest told Col. Edmund W. Rucker, one of his five brigade commanders, "When we strike them they will not know how few men are here. Their cavalry will move out ahead of the infantry, and should reach the crossroads three hours in advance." Forrest believed he could "whip" the Union cavalry here and by the time the infantry came up to support the cavalry, they would be "so tired out we will ride right over them."[6]

Both forces were converging on Brice's Cross Roads, four miles west of Baldwyn and the Mobile and Ohio Railroad. Here was the juncture of the Ripley-Fulton Road and the road from Baldwyn to Pontotoc. The two-story Brice home stood at the crossroads. One half mile to the northwest, the Ripley-Fulton Road crossed Tishomingo Creek on a narrow wooden bridge. On the 10th at 4 A.M., Forrest began moving his forces. The Union cavalry led by Forrest's old adversary Brig. Gen. Benjamin Grierson, began to ride toward the crossroads at 5:30. The infantry, meanwhile, was still in camp eating their breakfast and did not begin their march until 7 A.M. This separation of the Union forces was exactly the situation Forrest sought.[7]

Grierson crossed Tishomingo Creek and reached Brice's Cross Roads at 9:45, after brushing aside a small force of Confederates sent there to watch the junction. He pursued these men north-east toward Baldwin. About a mile from the crossroads, he ran into the advance of Brig. Gen. Hylan B. Lyon's brigade of eight hundred men. Just as the skirmishers deployed, Forrest rode up with his escort and took command on the field. The Battle of Brice's Cross Roads had begun.[8]

At this point Forrest asked Lyon not to fully commit to an attack but to probe the Union forces. He sent word back for Col. Tyree H. Bell. He said, "Tell Bell to move up fast and fetch all he's got." Both sides were now fighting on foot. With his usual bulldog tenacity, Forrest now had Lyon's men come into action fully by charging the enemy. His intention was to deceive the Union commander and make him believe that the Confederates had more men at the front. The Union commander called the charge "extremely fierce" and thought he was facing four thousand men instead of eight hundred. Again Forrest's belief that "one man in motion was worth two standing to receive and attack" was put into practice, and he succeeded.[9]

The thick woods and the posturing by Forrest's men, however, would not fool the Union leadership for long, and after an hour the Confederates withdrew back to the edge of the woods. Fortunately for Forrest, Col. Edmund W. Rucker arrived after an eighteen-mile march from Booneville with his seven-hundred-man brigade. Col. William A. Johnson's five-hundred-man brigade also arrived, and both were placed to the left of Lyon's men. Forrest now had two-thirds the number of men that Grierson had.[10]

After the Confederates withdrew to the woods, Grierson communicated with Sturgis and his infantry column. He wrote that he "had an advantageous position and could hold it if the infantry was brought up promptly." At this point, Sturgis's men had marched five miles and halted for the wagon train to catch up on the almost impassable roads. After receiving Grierson's note, Sturgis dispatched his forward-most brigade commander to move up his men "as rapidly as possible without distressing his troops."[11]

Forrest continued his holding action, and at 1 p.m. General Buford arrived with the artillery and Bell's brigade. Forrest now had all the men he would have this day. Preferring to attack, Forrest once said that he would "give more for fifteen minutes of bulge on the enemy than for a week of tactics." Forrest, thus far, even with inferior numbers had maintained the "bulge" for three hours.[12]

The Union forces were brought up from the rear as quickly as possible. They began arriving at about 1:30. The Union cavalry holding the crossroads were now growing tired. As the infantry arrived, "They were already half-broken from the hardships of the ten days' march and enervated by the great heat." Strung out for a long distance, many had dropped out of rank long before they arrived on the battlefield. When they did arrive, they were "exhausted and spiritless."[13]

In the early afternoon, for a short time, the battlefield was remarkably quiet as both sides repositioned troops. Forrest now was ready to begin his attack in earnest. He immediately deployed his artillery against the semicircle of Union troops arcing across the crossroads. Feeling that he had beaten the Union cavalry, he could now take care of the infantry. Forrest rode along the center of his lines on his big sorrel horse. He rode with his "saber in hand, sleeves rolled up, his coat lying on the pommel of his saddle, looking like the very God of War." Encouraging his troops, he shouted, "Get up, men. I have ordered Bell to charge on the left. When you hear his guns, and the bugle sounds, every man must charge, and we will give them hell."[14]

Bell's brigade on the Confederate left advanced through brush so thick that they moved to within thirty yards of the Yankees before they began their assault. The battle was savage. As Forrest's men advanced toward the crossroads in the thick underbrush, their lines shortened, giving them more cohesion. Bell, on the left, met a tremendous fire from the Union soldiers, causing part of his command to fall back. The Union commander, observing this weakness, tried to move his men forward to break the Confederate line. Forrest recognized this disastrous development, dismounted, and called his two escort companies to tie their horses and follow him. Forrest's quick action, the support of his escort, and the succor of a nearby reserve of 280 men checked the Union advance.[15]

Toward the center of the Confederate line, Rucker was also challenged with fixed bayonets as the Union infantry advanced. Rucker, not willing to abandon such hard-fought ground, shouted, "Kneel on the ground, men, draw your six shooters, and don't run!" The Union troops met the Confederates in fierce hand-to-hand fighting but could not break through; the Union bayonets were no equal to Rucker's pistols.[16]

It was at this point in the battle that Union fortune shifted from bad to worse. The push by the Union in the center withered under the steady firepower of the Confederates. Just as the fighting reached a crescendo on the Confederate extreme right, the 2nd Tennessee Calvary Regiment under Col. Clark R. Barteau crashed through the woods, driving off a Union cavalry force on their left flank. Barteau, now in the Federal rear, deployed his 250 men in a long line to exaggerate his numbers. To complement the ruse, his bugler rode up and down the line sounding the charge from different points, while his men kept up a hot fire on the Union forces.[17]

Forrest now wished to put as much pressure as possible on the Union troops and took a great risk with his artillery. Forrest called to Morton and pointed to a column of Confederates moving to the front. He told Morton that he was going to lead the column and strike the Union forces and "double'em up on the road." He instructed Morton to take his artillery and "charge right down the road, and get as close as you can. Give 'em hell right up yonder where I am going to double 'em up." As the bugle sounded, Morton moved his guns down the road at a gallop. At sixty yards he halted and ordered the guns into action. At the short range the Union forces could not stand both the artillery barrage and the Confederate assault.[18]

It was now after 4 P.M., and the Union forces began to withdraw. The Confederates broke through the woods into the clear-

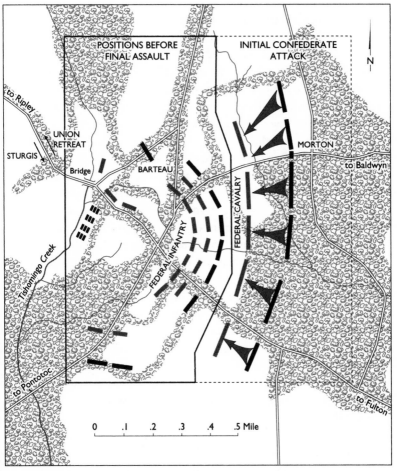

Battle of Brice's Cross Roads, Mississippi, June 10, 1864. *Bill Nelson*

ing around the Brice house, and along the entire Union front, the army "drifted to the rear, and was soon altogether beyond control." Sturgis wrote, "Order soon gave way to confusion and confusion to panic."[19]

Sturgis tried to rally his men and stop the retreat by deploying the Third Brigade under the command of Col. Edward Bouton. This brigade comprised three regiments of African Americans who had remained in the rear to protect the wagon train. These men were formed and held their defensive positions and fell back five times. They, however, took many casualties and were overwhelmed by their own troops trying to escape the battlefield, "crowding in like an avalanche."[20]

Adding to the chaos at the crossroads was the large wagon train. Most of the wagons were driven across Tishomingo Creek and pointed toward the Union lines. In the attempt to turn the teams of four and six mules back toward the bridge, they crowded together, creating even more panic. The uncaptured Union artillery went flying ahead of the wagons over the narrow bridge. The Confederates, now attacking with vigor, caused the teamsters to abandon their wagons and set some on fire. In panic, some men even cut the teams out of their harnesses, mounted the animals, and rode hell-bent to the rear. As the Confederates came up, they saw wagons, ambulances, and guns with their caissons "in utter disorder." The road was "beaten into mud," and the big army wagons were stuck blocking the way for those trying to escape the Confederate assault.[21]

Forrest was at his best in pursuit, and he did not relent. He pushed Buford's troops forward to keep pressure on the Union rear while he, his escort, and Bell's men took another road in an attempt to reach Salem, Mississippi. He hoped to get ahead of the Union mob, which had become a "hell of a stampede." Forrest continued his attack for the next two days, pursuing Sturgis's men for more than fifty miles. Sturgis's shattered command limped into Memphis on the 15th. [22]

Forrest fought and defeated a Union force nearly three times the size of his forces. They inflicted casualties of 223 killed, 394 wounded, and 1,623 missing (mostly captured). Forrest's chief surgeon reported 96 killed and 396 wounded. But Forrest and his men also captured 16 pieces of artillery, nearly 200 wagons and ambulances, 1,500 stand, of small arms and 300,000 rounds of ammunition.[23]

The defeat of Sturgis bewildered Sherman, who wrote to Secretary of War Edwin M. Stanton, "I cannot understand how he [Forrest] could defeat Sturgis with 8,000 men." He also wrote, "I will have the matter of Sturgis critically examined . . . I cannot but believe he had troops enough." He wrote further, "Forrest is the very devil, and I think he has got some of our troops under cower." Sherman planned to send Maj. Gen. Andrew J. Smith and Brig. Gen. Joseph A. Mower into the field and, if necessary, to "follow Forrest to the death, if it cost 10,000 lives and breaks the Treasury. There will never be peace in Tennessee till Forrest is dead."[24]

The victory at Brice's Cross Roads altered Union strategy. Instead of sending troops to operate against Mobile, Alabama, Smith was sent to Memphis. Also, other troops remained in Decatur and Huntsville rather than marching to reinforce Sherman in Atlanta. The Union leadership, however, would now be more earnest in prosecuting the war and tasked Smith with occupying Forrest and "devastating the land over which he has passed or may pass."[25]

Smith did not dally in his effort to strike at Forrest. On July 5, 11,000 infantry, 3,200 cavalry, and 500 artillerymen moved out of La Grange, Tennessee. The column moved southward and arrived just north of Ripley, Mississippi, on the 7th. Learning of the movement of this large force, Forrest and Stephen Lee rode to look for ground suitable to make a stand against the approaching Federal army. Forrest during this time was suffering from boils, which "greatly depleted even his iron constitution."[26]

Smith moved through Ripley and burned churches and other principal buildings, leaving a "broad belt of smoke and flame" ten miles wide. Forrest realized he needed to delay Smith, but knew his command was not ready to engage this overwhelming Union force. He sent Buford's and Chalmers's divisions to determine the enemy's strength but not to engage the Union column.[27]

A brief clash at Pontotoc on the 12th temporarily stopped the Union advance. Instead of moving against the Confederates the next day, Smith used his cavalry as a diversion and on the 13th moved east toward Tupelo instead of south to Okolona as both Lee and Forrest had hoped. This change of direction confused the Confederates, and they left the road to Tupelo unguarded. Smith now had no Confederates in his front, and Forrest felt compelled to attack the Union rear while Buford and Chalmers used parallel roads to attack Smith's flanks. These attacks were brushed off with few casualties, and Grierson's cavalry was in Tupelo by noon. After tearing up the tracks of the Mobile and Ohio Railroad both north and south of the town, Smith reversed his march, headed west, and arrived in Harrisburg at 9 that night.[28]

Forrest had spent the day nipping at the heels of the Federal force and arrived near Harrisburg after sunset. After a short rest, Forrest decided to ride and reconnoiter the Union lines about a mile distant. He and one of his staff officers hadn't ridden far before Forrest realized he had forgotten his pistols. His aide offered one of his, but Forrest declined, saying he did not think it would be needed. In the dark, however, the two blundered into Union wagons and teams. The darkness obscured their uniforms, and they rode through much of the enemy camp. On their way back through the lines, however, they were halted by two Union soldiers on picket duty. Thinking quickly, Forrest rode up to them and in an angry tone said, "How dare you halt your commanding officer?" Forrest and his aide then spurred their horses and crouched, expecting to be fired upon. Shots from the pickets fell wide, and the two returned safely to the Confederate lines.[29]

During the ride, Forrest observed an enemy force that was "strongly posted and prepared to give battle." With Smith in this strong defensive position, Forrest preferred to wait for him to move and attack his strung-out columns. Lee, however, was feeling pressure from his superiors to deal with Smith quickly so that his troops could relieve other points then being threatened by attack, particularly Mobile.[30]

On the 14th Forrest was in the field early awaiting Lee's orders. Lee had about 7,500 men available to face Smith's 11,000 entrenched Federals, supported by six batteries and Grierson's cavalry of 3,200 men at the rear and left flank. Forrest's forces included Buford's 3,200-man division posted on the left, Chalmers's division of 2,300 that occupied the center, and Brig. Gen. Philip D. Roddey's 1,500-man division that anchored the right.

At 8 A.M., under a cloudless sky, Buford's three brigades, with a rebel yell, rushed toward the Union lines across a rising slope. The Union troops withheld their fire and then unleashed "a scorching fire" of small arms and artillery. The Confederate lines reached the Union earthworks, fought desperately for a few minutes, but were repulsed with high casualties. Seeing the disorganized withdrawal, Forrest rushed up to his men, "seized their colors, and after a short appeal ordered them to form a new line." Forrest, however, realized that a further charge would be useless. The Union forces used this time to push out beyond their entrenchments. They quickly drove off or captured all the Confederates nearby. By 10:30, after a series of brave but uncoordinated charges, the battle was over. The fierceness of the fighting can be attested to by the fact that in front of the Union lines more than two hundred of Forrest's men lay dead. More than one thousand were wounded while the Union suffered only seven hundred casualties.[31]

S. D. Lee wrote no contemporary report of the battle. Thirty-seven years after the event, he wrote that Forrest had changed the plan of battle. He questioned why he had not sent Roddey forward. Forrest had claimed that "Buford's right had been rashly thrown forward and repulsed. In the exercise of my discretion I did not move Roddey forward but moved him to the left, and formed a new line." Lee then told Forrest that "in doing as you did, you failed to carry out the plan of battle agreed on." But Lee also admitted, "I am sure he [Forrest] did the best as he saw it."[32]

That night Smith put the torch to houses in Harrisburg. Low on rations and ammunition, he ordered his troops to make ready to return to Memphis. On the 15th, with characteristic vigor, Forrest attacked the Union rear as it moved out of its encampment. As Forrest rode across a field while directing the pursuit, he was struck in the foot by a bullet, producing a "painful wound." Carried to the rear, he sent word for Chalmers to take command.[33]

The news of Forrest's wounding spread quickly through the Confederate ranks. The word passed along the lines that he had died. After the wound was dressed, Forrest mounted his horse and in his shirtsleeves galloped among his men to show them he was well. One witness claimed that the "effect produced upon the men by the appearance of General Forrest is indescribable. They seemed wild with joy at seeing their great leader was still with them." Rumors in the Union camps also circulated that Forrest was dead. Sherman wrote, "Is Forrest surely dead? If so, tell General Mower I am pledged to him for his promotion, and if Old Abe don't make good my promise then General Mower may have my place.[34]

Smith's column was only lightly harassed as it made its way north. He arrived in La Grange on July 21 and in Memphis a couple of days later, after just over two weeks in the field. Smith had more success against Forrest than anyone had in several years. Furthermore, he kept Forrest occupied while Sherman continued his advance on Atlanta. Smith's mission had been to destroy Forrest, yet he had not accomplished what Sherman had asked. Sherman, therefore, ordered Smith back into the field "to pursue and continue to follow Forrest . . . till recalled by me or General Grant."[35]

Before Smith could begin another campaign, he had repairs made on the Memphis and Charleston Railroad and on the Mississippi Central Railroad in order to better move troops and supplies against Forrest. On July 28, Smith began to move portions of his command toward Grand Junction. His 18,000-man column headed south toward Columbus, Mississippi. From here he planned to march northeast to Decatur, Alabama.[36]

Forrest, still suffering from his foot wound, had just gotten back in the saddle, having commanded his troops from a buggy since being wounded. Forrest now had a new department commander, Maj. Gen. Dabney H. Maury of Virginia. Dabney had great respect for Forrest and wrote him upon taking command, "I intrust upon you the operations against the enemy . . . I would not . . . interfere with your plan for conducting these operations." He added, "It is with no small satisfaction I reflect that of all the commanders in the Confederacy you are accustomed to accomplish the very greatest results with small means when left to your untrammeled judgement."[37]

Smith, meanwhile, had moved his men by rail to Holly Springs and on August 8 started south to the Tallahatchie River. After crossing this body of water, he continued south and on August 10 occupied Oxford, Mississippi, after a brief skirmish with Confederate troops led by Chalmers. The Union forces, however, stayed there only a day and then marched north, back to Abbeville, near the Tallahatchie crossing where they bivouacked late that night.[38]

Forrest continued his pursuit, bringing two brigades and Morton's artillery. They arrived in Oxford from Pontotoc at 11 P.M., just hours after the Union soldiers left. He immediately sent word for his commands to gather. A week of steady rain left both sides content to watch each other. Forrest knew that he could not defeat Smith's overwhelming force, and he decided to try a bold strike on Memphis with hopes that Smith would quit his campaign.

On August 18, in a downpour, Forrest gathered two thousand of the best men and horses (about half his force) and led them westward out of town. Through knee-deep mud and swollen streams, they rode as hard as they could. By 7 A.M. on the 19th, they reached Panola, where the Tennessee and Mississippi Railroad crosses the Tallahatchie River. Leaving some one hundred unfit men behind, he continued his ride northward.[39]

While Forrest rode toward Memphis, Chalmers remained active at Oxford to bluff Smith. On Saturday the 20th, Forrest arrived at Hernando, only 25 miles south of Memphis. At 3 A.M. on August 21, after a short rest, Forrest led the 1,500 men who were still able to keep up toward the outskirts of Memphis.[40]

As they rode toward the city, Confederate scouts provided Forrest with reports covering the most current information on troops and the fortifications. With this information, Forrest formulated his plan of attack. He chose his brother Capt. William Forrest and his Forty Scouts to take the advance. They were to capture the enemy's pickets without firing a shot. After this, they were to ride to the headquarters of Maj. Gen. Stephen A. Hurlbut and capture him and his headquarters. A second force followed William to hold the main crossroads in the city and capture any transports in the river. A third detachment would engage Union troops in the suburbs. His other brother Lt. Col. Jesse Forrest and a hand-picked detachment was to capture Maj. Gen. Cadwallader Washburn. A fourth detachment would attack another outlying Union encampment. Bedford Forrest, with the artillery and other detachments, would remain outside the city to cover the withdrawal of the four raiding parties.[41]

The Confederate troops moved forward at dawn. William Forrest succeeded in reaching the picket post and capturing the pickets. A single rifle shot, however, alerted the second post, and William decided to ride past them. In a state of excitement, they swept into the city with a rebel yell. This small band reached the Gayoso House Hotel, and Bill Forrest rode his horse into the lobby. Unfortunately, he failed to capture Hurlbut, who had slept elsewhere that night.[42]

Jesse Forrest did no better. Washburn, warned of the approaching Confederates, scurried to Fort Pickering just south of town. Jesse and his band captured some staff officers and Washburn's uniform. Hurlbut could not help but later write, "After the event they removed me from command because I could not keep Forrest out of West Tennessee, and now Washburn can't keep him out of his own bedroom!"[43]

The city was now in chaos. The Union soldiers and the city's militia began to rally and take defensive measures. Bedford Forrest struck the Union flank with his escort and men from Bell's brigade. By this time, his small force had done all it could, and the recall was sounded at 9. The Confederates fled the town with six hundred prisoners. A pursuit led by Union Col. Mathew Starr of the Sixth Illinois Cavalry overtook the rear of the Confederates south of the town. Forrest turned to meet Starr in a saber duel and mortally wounded the Union colonel.[44]

Forrest rode south toward Hernando. Many of the six hundred prisoners in tow were convalescing soldiers who had fled into the streets after the alarm was raised and fell into Confederate hands. Most of the others had little clothing or no shoes. This slowed the escape, and Forrest dispatched a flag of truce to exchange the prisoners for those of his command who had been taken that morning, with the promise that the rest of the Union soldiers would be released on parole. If the enemy rejected this offer, he would wait for clothing for the men. During the parole meeting, one Union officer told Forrest that Washburn had said, "He will catch you before you get back." Forrest told the officer, "You may tell the general from me . . . that I am going back by the same road I came by, and if we meet, I promise to whip him out of his boots." General Washburn claimed that he had no authority to exchange prisoners, but he did provide clothing. Forrest eventually paroled two hundred of the men too infirm to make the march south.[45]

Smith learned at noon on the 22nd that Forrest had attacked Memphis. Smith never even realized that Forrest had ridden north. Chalmers, whose instructions from Forrest were to keep Smith occupied, did a convincing job. Smith, however, had five thousand cavalry and might have engaged Forrest and his weary command before he could ride south and rejoin Chalmers. Smith instead, on the 22nd, again occupied Oxford and this time burned much of the town. On the 25th, he and his column recrossed the Tallahatchie on their way back to Memphis.[46]

Smith lost a key opportunity to cripple or destroy Forrest on his retreat. The entire campaign had cost Forrest about thirty-five casualties while he inflicted about eighty on the Union forces. The capture of the prisoners was a blow to the Union, and the raid ended Smith's foray into Mississippi. Yet the entire campaign had succeeded strategically for the Union. Forrest had not been able to ride into Georgia and Tennessee to wreck havoc on Sherman's communications.

Chapter 6

"That Devil Forrest"

T HE DEPARTMENT OF ALABAMA, Mississippi,
and East Louisiana received a new commanding officer in August. Lt. Gen. Richard Taylor met in Meridian with Forrest to
discuss future operations. He described Bedford as a "tall, stal-
wart man, with grayish hair, mild countenance, and slow and
homely of speech." On September 2, Atlanta had fallen and
Gen. John B. Hood, in command of the Army of Tennessee, was
moving northward to strike into Tennessee and Kentucky. In order to support General Hood, then west of Atlanta, Forrest was
ordered to move his cavalry north of the Tennessee River to
strike at Sherman's communications.[1]

In their initial meeting, Forrest asked Taylor about his route
of advance and retreat if pressed by the enemy. He also wanted
to know about logistical matters, how he would get supplies, and
what he would do with prisoners. Taylor at first believed Forrest
timid but later realized that Forrest was merely shaping the campaign in his mind. Bedford called for the superintendent of the
railway and asked him some questions. Immediately Forrest's
manner changed. "In a dozen sharp sentences he told his wants,

[and] said he would leave a staff officer to bring up his supplies." He then informed Taylor that he "hoped to give an account of himself in Tennessee."[2]

It was nearly two weeks before Forrest could assemble his troops and supplies for a march northward. During this time, Forrest carefully pondered every contingency. During these periods, he often sat "immobile, chin sunk on chest, or walked head down with his hands clasped behind him beneath the tails of his coat." While planning this campaign, he walked in circles at the railroad station at West Point, Mississippi. One man, demanding that Forrest listen to a grievance, continued to interrupt the general as he strolled along the platform. Forrest finally heard enough and, hardly looking up, struck the man with his fist, "knocked the man out and kept right on his rounds, calmly and unconsciously stepping over the prostrate body as he came round again."[3]

On September 16, Forrest moved out of Verona, Mississippi, with Buford's division, a brigade from Chalmer's division, and two batteries of artillery—a total of 3,542 men. About 450 dismounted men and the artillery went by rail to Corinth. By the evening of the 19th, his whole force was in Cherokee Station, Alabama, about thirty-five miles east of Corinth. Here they remained for thirty-six hours, cooking rations and shoeing horses until they moved toward the Tennessee River on the 21st.[4]

The next day, Forrest's column passed through Florence and was joined by about one thousand men, four hundred of whom had no horses. Forrest sent detachments on a night ride to cut the telegraph wires at McDonald's Station on the Tennessee and Alabama Railroad, about seven miles south of Athens, Alabama. On the 23rd, the main column moved to Athens and arrived late in the afternoon. After driving in the Union pickets, Forrest sent a small force to the north side of town to cut the telegraph wires and to stop trains from leaving the town. He encircled Athens and positioned his artillery to hammer away at the Federals who had retreated into a substantial blockhouse fort south of the town.[5]

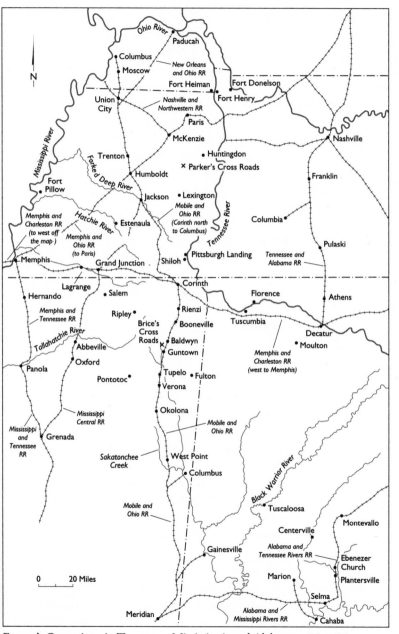

Forrest's Operations in Tennessee, Mississippi, and Alabama, 1864–1865.
Bill Nelson

A heavy rain fell all night, and on the morning of the 24th, Forrest consumed three hours preparing for the attack and testing his artillery on the defenses. Just after 10:30 A.M., Forrest sent in a flag of truce asking for unconditional surrender. The Federal commander, Col. Wallace Campbell, refused. Forrest then sent in a note requesting to meet personally with Campbell. Forrest told the colonel that he had eight thousand men, enough to carry the works, and that he wished to avoid bloodshed. Forrest also told Campbell he would show him his forces. Once again using bluff, Forrest began shifting troops and artillery to deceive his adversary. This ploy fooled Campbell, and he agreed to surrender his command.[6]

While Forrest entertained Campbell, reinforcements for the garrison arrived south of Athens by rail. Forrest's men cut them off and surrounded the 350-man force. After an hour of fighting and with more than a hundred casualties, they also surrendered. During the fight, Jesse Forrest was severely wounded in the thigh.[7]

A few miles north of Athens, Forrest encountered another blockhouse. The Union officer in charge "defiantly refused' to surrender after Forrest deployed his artillery. The refusal angered Forrest and "he made the atmosphere blue for a while." After calming himself, he asked one of his officers, "Does the d——d fool want to be blown up? . . . Well, I'll blow him up then. Give him hell, Captain Morton." Morton's first shot struck near the top of the structure, tearing away a large log. The second shot went between two of the logs and sent dust, shingles, and planks flying. Immediately a small white cloth showed from one of the openings. Captain Morton ordered a cease-fire only to hear from Forrest, "Keep it up. . . . It'll take a sheet to attract my eye at this distance." A few more rounds brought out a much larger flag of truce.[8]

The day's work netted Forrest a large bounty. It included about 1,300 prisoners, 2 locomotives, 2 trains with their locomotives, 2 12-pound howitzers, 38 wagons, 4 ambulances, 1,000 stand of arms, hundreds of horses, and large quantities of stores and ammunition. His loss was 5 killed and 25 wounded. After burning the bridges, military buildings, the blockhouses, and all the stores and supplies he could not carry, Forrest continued northward.[9]

The following day, Sunday the 25th, the Confederates advanced to Sulphur Springs. They encountered two well-built blockhouses and an earthwork that guarded a trestle. This trestle was the most important segment of the tracks for miles because it spanned a deep ravine, that rose more than seventy feet high and stretched more than 300 feet. Forrest carefully moved his troops close to the Union defenses while Morton positioned his artillery to command the Union earthworks. After accomplishing this, Forrest demanded the surrender of the garrison. An hour passed before the answer arrived—the demand was rejected.[10]

Forrest ordered Morton to open fire on the enemy. At eight hundred yards, Morton began shelling the works. In two hours, he threw in eight hundred rounds, dismounted the Union guns, killed the commanding officer, and left the "dead and dying lying thick along the works." Yet the Union earthworks showed no inclination to surrender. Forrest would not allow the carnage to continue and sent in another flag of truce demanding surrender. This time the garrison acceded.[11]

Here Forrest captured over 800 men, 300 horses, 20 wagons and teams, and large amounts of commissary and ordnance stores. This fight, however, spent so much of his ammunition that he had to send four pieces of his artillery and the captured guns back to Florence, Alabama. Forrest sent Buford on ahead with a brigade, and the rest of his men went to work cutting down the trestle and setting the timbers afire. This kept them occupied through the night.[12]

Advancing on Pulaski, Forrest found little resistance. The blockhouse at the Elk River was abandoned, and the blockhouse at Richland Creek, defended by 50 soldiers, surrendered after a short fight. On the 27th, as he approached Pulaski, he was met by stubborn resistance outside the town. The Confederates drove in the Union force but found the defenses too formidable to attack. That night Forrest had his men build campfires and deceptively put out a picket line close to the enemy's fortifications. Then his men quietly formed up and rode east toward Fayetteville to strike the Nashville and Chattanooga Railroad at Tullahoma.[13]

On the 28th Forrest's column reached Fayetteville. He sent two small detachments to cut the telegraph lines north and south of Tullahoma. They camped five miles from Fayetteville that night and moved on Tullahoma the next morning. Reaching Mulberry at noon, he learned from citizens and his scouts that overwhelming Union forces were beginning to approach Atlanta, Chattanooga, and other points. With his artillery ammunition nearly exhausted, his forces drained by sending back men to guard both his prisoners and the captured property, Forrest believed it imprudent to continue his advance.[14]

Forrest turned southward and split his force. He sent Buford and 1,500 men to strike at Huntsville, Alabama, and the Memphis and Charleston Railroad. Forrest took the rest of his command westward in "an obscure, circuitous road to Lewisburg" to confuse the enemy. On October 1, he captured Spring Hill and, moving toward Columbia, captured blockhouses and burned bridges. The following day, he continued southward to escape the Union columns trying to surround him. Riding toward Florence, Forrest sent units out to slow the Union advance.[15]

On the 5th, his force began crossing the Tennessee River. Forrest took the last boat to safety and expected every man to take his turn at the oars and poles. When he observed a lieutenant in the bow of his boat taking no part, he asked, "Why don't you take hold of an oar or a pole and help get this boat across?" The lieutenant replied that officers did not do this work when enlisted men were present to perform this duty. Forrest, who was himself propelling the boat, flew into a rage. With his pole, he struck the lieutenant and knocked him into the water. After he was pulled back into the boat, Forrest said, "Now, damn you, get hold of the oars and go to work! If I knock you out of the boat again, I'll let you drown."[16]

Forrest had escaped again. This foray had cost the Union 2,360 prisoners and another 1,000 casualties. He destroyed some key Union defenses and rail lines with losses of 47 killed and 293 wounded. Forrest also captured 800 horses, 7 guns, 50 wagons, 2,000 stand of arms and large amounts of commissary medical and ordnance supplies. But Forrest was thoroughly worn out. He wrote Taylor that his "strength is failing and it is absolutely necessary that I should have some rest."[17]

Forrest, however, could not stay out of the saddle for long. He suggested operations along the Tennessee River to strike at the Union's waterborne logistical artery. Forrest set Buford's division in motion and ordered Chalmers to meet him in Jackson, Tennessee, with as many men as they could muster. Many of his men were allowed to make short trips back to their homes to procure fresh mounts and clothing. By mid-October, he brought his forces together and began moving north toward Jackson.[18]

Early on the 29th, Forrest arrived at Fort Heiman, at the fork of the Tennessee and Big Sandy Rivers. Here he found his batteries built and his men ready to attack Union transports. The Union forces had no idea that Forrest and his men were present until the 184-ton steamship *Mazeppa* with two barges in tow passed the lower guns. The Confederates opened fire and within minutes disabled the vessel. The *Mazeppa,* however, ran aground across the river, and her crew escaped. A rebel swimmer crossed the river and brought a skiff back with a line, and the Confederates warped the steamboat across the river. The prize contained hardtack, shoes, blankets, and clothing. Before the Confederates could finish unloading the vessel, three Union gunboats appeared. Forrest decided to burn the *Mazeppa* rather than let her fall back into Union hands.[19]

The following day, the steamer *Anna* was spotted headed down the river. When she came abreast of the artillery, the Confederates fired a volley, and she hove to and ran up a white flag. She then turned toward the bank, and the Confederates began to rush toward the edge of the water. As she neared the bank, however, she crowded steam and shot down river. The artillerist ran back to the guns and got off a few shots, but she escaped.[20]

Several hours later, the 179-ton stern-wheel naval gunboat *Undine* appeared. She had earlier accompanied the *Anna* but had returned to Johnsonville before the rebels attacked. Her commanding officer heard the artillery fire, cleared his ship for action, and headed back downstream. Forrest's men allowed the *Undine* to steam past the upper battery and then opened fire. At seven hundred yards, the *Undine* returned fire with her eight twenty-four-pounders. She fought for nearly an hour, until a Confederate shell disabled her. As she floated out of range, her crew repaired the damage, and she steamed back into the fight.[21]

Just as the *Undine* entered the fray for the second time, the army transport *Venus* hove into sight. Despite receiving signals of danger, she continued downriver and anchored beside the *Undine.* Twenty minutes later, a third transport, the *J. W. Cheeseman,* towing a barge, also passed down the river and like the *Venus* did not heed the warnings. *Venus* was quickly disabled and floated to the west bank of the river. The Confederates shifted their guns and within an hour forced the *Undine* to run ashore and forced the *Venus* to surrender shortly thereafter.[22]

The *Undine* and *Venus* were made ready for Confederate service. Forrest's men found the *Cheeseman* too damaged to repair and set her on fire. Confederate flags now flew from ships on the Tennessee River for the first time since 1862.[23]

The gunboats, protected by Forrest's men ashore, began moving toward Johnsonville. Heavy rain slowed the troops, and the gunboats forged ahead. On the afternoon of November 2, six miles below Johnsonville, Forrest's "horse marines" met the U.S. Navy. The *Venus* had steamed well in advance of the *Undine* and encountered the side-wheel gunboat *Tawah* and the stern-wheel gunboat *Key West.* Both of these vessels were more heavily armed, and they quickly overwhelmed the cavalry soldiers, who drove the *Venus* ashore and escaped through the woods. The *Undine* steamed to help the *Venus,* but arrived too late, and was driven off and escaped downriver.[24]

Forrest's men ashore arrived at the outskirts of Johnsonville on the 3d. Here Forrest deployed his artillery and troops without notice. He planned to stop any Union gunboats from reinforcing the Union positions, as he bombarded Johnsonville to destroy the numerous transports, the large warehouse crammed with valuable supplies and the acres of army stores.[25]

At 8 A.M. on November 4, six Union gunboats stood up the river from Paducah to deal with the *Undine*. They immediately came under fire from the batteries Forrest placed on the river. At nearly the same time, three Union gunboats above Forrest's positions steamed downriver. The Union gunboats completely outmatched the *Undine*, and the Confederates destroyed and abandoned her. Forrest's batteries along the bank, however, maintained a scathing fire on the naval vessels and kept the six gunboats from running up the river to join the others.[26]

While the rebel batteries held off these warships, the other batteries were being readied to bombard the wharves, the transports, and the depot in Johnsonville. At 2, ten guns opened on the transports and wharves. The ships and facilities were set on fire, and that night "the wharf for nearly one mile up and down the river presented one solid sheet of flame."[27]

Forrest accomplished his mission and that night moved six miles south "by the light of the enemy's burning property." His column reached Corinth on November 10. Forrest claimed only eleven casualties. He destroyed four gunboats, fourteen transports, twenty barges, and the Johnsonville depot. He also captured 26 pieces of artillery and 150 prisoners and, after supplying his command with captured property, turned over to the quartermaster 9,000 pairs of shoes and 1,000 blankets. His estimate of the Union losses was over $6 million.[28]

Forrest had become an almost mythical character. His ability to take a small force deep into enemy territory and escape won him quite a reputation. After this strike on Johnsonville, telegrams sent from the North had him spotted from Canada to Chicago and Michigan City. Agitated, Sherman wrote "that devil Forrest was down about Johnsonville and was making havoc among the gun-boats and transports." After the war, Sherman wrote that this was a "feat of arms which, I confess, excited my admiration."[29]

Forrest had not even reached Johnsonville and made his raid before he was issued instructions to operate with General Hood. It had been almost exactly a year since his superiors had detached him from the Army of Tennessee to operate with more independence. Placed in command of Hood's cavalry, he received another division and a portion of a brigade. The troops and their mounts, however, were worn out, and the units' numbers were depleted. Many of the men, on furloughs to their homes to gather new mounts, had not returned. He had, in effect, only five thousand men.[30]

Hood was engaged in a desperate gamble to invade Tennessee, with hopes of drawing Union troops from the Deep South and stopping Sherman's advance through Georgia toward Savannah. Hood, if successful, hoped to continue advancing through Kentucky and maybe into the North. Hood placed Forrest in front of his three columns of soldiers as they advanced northward. The invasion started ominously. On November 21, as Forrest broke camp, a snowstorm and then a hard freeze hit. As the columns advanced, the roads turned to mush, slowing his men to a crawl.[31]

With Hood on the move, the Union troops began to concentrate and rushed reinforcements into Tennessee. Maj. Gen. John Schofield at Pulaski realized that he might be cut off and retreated toward Columbia, Tennessee. Forrest's men harassed the Union soldiers and "almost constantly" skirmished with Schofield's forces as they fled northward. Schofield reached Columbia before Forrest and joined Brig. Gen. Jacob D. Cox's division. They held the town while Forrest pressured the Union positions until Hood's force could arrive. Hood managed to reach Columbia on the 27th of November. The Union troops marched north that night and got across the Duck River early the next morning, leaving the Confederates once again trying to catch and defeat the Union army.[32]

On the 29th, the Union infantry fell back toward Franklin, and Forrest decided to push his men forward to Spring Hill. At this point, Hood might have cut off Schofield's retreat. Late on the afternoon of the 29th, Forrest realized this and about a mile and a half outside of Spring Hill, he sent Chalmers to probe the Union positions. Advancing on what he thought were only small detachments of cavalry, Chalmers was repulsed with a scathing fire. Forrest now knew he had met the main Union column and remarked to Chalmers, "They was in there sure enough, wasn't they, Chalmers?"[33]

Forrest, not satisfied that the Union force would hold its position, ordered another charge. The Confederates could not break the strongly defended lines and fell back. Forrest then dismounted his entire command "to push the enemy's right flank with all possible vigor." Hood, only two miles away, meanwhile, had reports of Forrest's contact with the enemy and sent word for him to hold his position "at all hazards." Forrest characteristically sent his men on the offensive to confuse the Union leadership regarding exactly what forces they faced.[34]

Maj. Gen. Patrick Cleburne's division arrived first to support Forrest and moved to the left. Forrest's and Cleburne's men were able to drive the Union soldiers out of their rifle pits toward Spring Hill. After General Cheatham arrived on the field, an uncoordinated attack created confusion and the Confederate forces lost their momentum, and heavy skirmishing continued throughout the night. Forrest, though, sent a small detachment to harass the Union forces at Thompson's Station, about five miles north of Spring Hill. At 11 P.M. he was able to create "much panic and confusion" among the Union forces but could not sustain the attack without support, and Federals moved past the Confederates toward Franklin. Hood, who had believed that the Union forces were trapped, missed a golden opportunity to isolate and defeat Schofield.[35]

Schofield reached Franklin on the morning of November 30 and quickly constructed defenses. Using the Harpeth River to anchor his left flank, Schofield manned crescent-shaped earthworks that commanded a hill with 20,000 of his 28,000 men. Hood and the Confederate army arrived just after noon and, against the advice of Forrest, attacked.

At 4:30 Hood's army made a frontal assault across two miles of rising open ground against the defenses. Forrest supported the assault with Chalmers on the left and Buford on the right. Schofield had detached two brigades in front of the defenses, the eighteen Confederate brigades sent forward quickly overwhelmed them, and the Union soldiers streamed back toward the defenses. The Union defenders hit the charging Confederates with a volley that struck down ranks of men as a scythe does wheat. Their momentum, however, carried them into the Union lines, but they could not sustain the attack and retreated. The rest of the Confederate attack did no better, being met with point-blank artillery and small arms fire. The battle continued until 9 that night. The carnage at Franklin cost Hood 6,200 men, including 6 generals dead, 5 wounded, and 1 captured. The Federal dead and wounded were only 2,326.

Hood's shattered army could only watch as Schofield moved out of Franklin that night to join Maj. Gen. Thomas in Nashville. Forrest did not suffer tremendous casualties and at dawn pursued the retreating Union columns. He harassed their rear but was unable to prevent Schofield's advance into Nashville. On the morning of December 2, Forrest's men were relieved by the infantry outside of Nashville and sent along with Maj. Gen. William B. Bates's division to attack Murfreesboro.

As Forrest marched toward Murfreesboro, he detached Col. D. C. Kelley to blockade the Cumberland River several miles below Nashville. On the 3d, they captured the transports *Prairie State* and *Prima Donna* loaded with horses, mules, and forage. Before they could get them unloaded, however, the ironclad *Carondelet* and four tinclads steamed down from Nashville and recaptured the transports.[36]

On his march Forrest destroyed railroad lines, bridges, blockhouses, and telegraph lines along the Nashville and Chattanooga Railroad toward Murfreesboro. Bates's division joined Forrest outside of Murfreesboro. The cavalry pressed ahead of Bates's men, driving in the pickets outside of the town on the 5th. Bates's infantry arrived the following day. Forrest ordered the infantry into line to attack. After a skirmish of two hours, the Yankee forces showed no inclination to fight outside the works. That night two more infantry brigades joined Forrest, bringing his force up to 6,500 men.[37]

On the 7th, the Union troops "moved out in strong force" beyond their defenses to fight the Confederates. They "moved boldly forward," driving back the Confederate pickets. Unexplainably, the Confederate infantry on the left broke and fled to the rear. Only one brigade stood its ground and could not stop the Federal advance. Forrest and Bates were "stunned," and both immediately rushed among the retreating soldiers to rally them. Forrest, with a combination of threats, curses, urging words, and commands, could not rally the men. As one of the color-bearers ran past Forrest, he grabbed the flag but could not stop the retreat. Forrest sent his aide to bring up two cavalry brigades with the words that the outcome of the battle depended on their promptness. They arrived, and these veteran troops charged the enemy and checked the advance.[38]

Following this battle Forrest continued his destruction of railroad tracks and prevented Union flanking movements. On the 13th his men captured a train of seventeen cars headed to Murfreesboro. On board were sixty thousand rations and a Union regiment. Forrest took the soldiers as prisoners but had to burn most of the rations, the cars, and the locomotive.[39]

General Thomas waited two weeks before moving 55,000 men of his 70,000-man army out of the trenches around Nashville. On December 15, he met Hood's crippled 30,000-man force on the outskirts of the city. Thomas sortied in a heavy fog and struck a devastating blow on the Confederates, who fell back into a defensive position during the night. The following day, in rain and snow, Thomas again hammered Hood. The Union cavalry gained his rear, and artillery pounded the Confederate positions. That afternoon the main assault broke the

Confederate army, and they fled in confusion. The Union suffered 3,062 casualties but inflicted 1,500 and captured another 4,500 prisoners.

On the night of the 16th Forrest learned of Hood's repulse and moved to protect the wrecked Confederate army. The advance, however, was difficult. His column had cattle, hogs, and prisoners, and most of Forrest's infantry was barefoot. They did reach the Duck River and crossed before the Union forces could come up on the 19th. During the crossing, as Forrest began to move his troops over the river, General Cheatham also arrived with his men and expected to cross first. Forrest rode up to Cheatham, explaining that he had arrived first and would cross ahead of Cheatham. Cheatham answered, "I think not, sir. You are mistaken. I intend to cross now, and will thank you to move out of the way of my troops." Forrest, never one to take abuse from anyone, drew his pistol and explained, "If you are a better man than I am, General Cheatham, your troops can cross ahead of mine." Lt. Gen. Stephen D. Lee, passing in a nearby ambulance, witnessed the disturbance and placated the officers before blood was spilled.[40]

Hood ordered Forrest, who had moved to Columbia, to hold the town as long as possible. Hood gave him an additional 1,900 men, 400 of whom did not have shoes and were not useful. The Union forces pushed across the Duck River on the morning of the 22d, and Forrest fell back south toward Pulaski and stopped on the night of December 23 at Lynnville. On the morning of the 24th, Forrest ordered his infantry up the pike north toward Columbia, and his cavalry advanced on their flanks. Three miles up the pike, they met the enemy, and after a "severe engagement," Forrest withdrew southward. The Union force came up and pressed Forrest until he crossed Richland Creek and reached Pulaski.[41]

On Christmas morning Forrest's men destroyed all the ammunition, train cars, and locomotives they could not get out of Pulaski. They moved out of the town and destroyed the bridge at Richland Creek. The Union troops continued to press Forrest's rear "with little intermission," and seven miles from Pulaski, on high ground, Forrest awaited the enemy. The Yankees had to march two miles through a narrow pass bounded by two high ridges that united to form a hill. Forrest placed his artillery on the hill to "sweep the hollow below an the road through it." Forrest then deployed his troops along the crest of the hill and on its flanks.[42]

At 1 P.M. Christmas Day, the Federal cavalry appeared, driving the Confederate rear guard through the pass. The Union commander halted his force, dismounted several regiments, and then advanced cautiously. The bluecoats were surprised by canister fire and volleys of musketry and fled in disorder. The Confederates charged down the hill after them, through the enemy's horses, and delivered another volley. The Union suffered 150 casualties and the loss of 50 prisoners, 300 cavalry horses, and an artillery piece. Forrest suffered fifteen killed and forty wounded.[43]

During the afternoon, the Federal cavalry column again approached, but now in sufficient strength to flank Forrest. Bad roads had delayed Forrest's withdrawal as his men pushed their horses through mud "belly-deep, and never less than up to their knees." The men, many still barefoot, had to march in ice, with sleet beating down on them. On the morning of the 26th, they managed to make fourteen miles and stopped at 1 A.M.[44]

At dawn the Union cavalry attacked again, determined to strike at Hood's rear before he could cross the Tennessee River. Fog shrouded the Confederate positions, and despite a deliberate advance the Union cavalry did not detect Forrest's men until they were nearly on top of them. A volley from the Confederates created "the wildest confusion." Forrest exacted another 150 casualties from the Union forces, captured 100 more prisoners and 150 cavalry horses, and killed as many as 400 of the enemy's horses. Fearing the Union column would strike again, he fell back in the fog, reached the Tennessee River on the evening of the 27th, and crossed without the Federals' attacking again.[45]

General Hood withdrew to Tuscumbia, and Forrest reported to him here. Recounting the sad shape of his men and horses and his inability to forage in this area, Hood approved Forrest's move to Corinth on the 30th. Forrest arrived on New Year's Day, and he furloughed Bell's brigade, allowing them to go to their homes for fresh horses and new clothing. A few days later, Rucker's brigade was given a similar furlough.[46]

Forrest's command would never recover. The Confederacy was in its death throes. Sherman had captured Savannah, and it would only be a short time before Robert E. Lee would abandon his defensive lines of Petersburg, Virginia. The Confederate army was also losing men in droves. Forrest moved his headquarters to Verona, about fifty-five miles south of Corinth, to recruit absentees and obtain more horses for his men. Forrest was to be assigned command of all the cavalry in the Departments of Alabama, Mississippi, and East Louisiana. Forrest now had ten thousand men in three states under his command. He was promoted to the rank of lieutenant general on February 28.[47]

Days earlier, Forrest had met with Union officers to discuss the exchange of prisoners and the possibility of the Union furnishing clothing and supplies for them. Meeting with Forrest at Rienzi, Mississippi, was Col. John G. Parkhurst and Capt. Lewis M. Hosea. Hosea, impressed by Forrest's "mental power" and his "quickness of perceptive comprehension," was during the meeting "frequently lost in real admiration." Hosea wrote that Forrest's language indicated a lack of education, but "his impressive manner conceals many otherwise noticeable defects." When Hosea presented Maj. Gen. James H. Wilson's compliments and his desire to meet Forrest in combat, Forrest said, "Jist tell Gin'ral Wilson that I know the nicest little place . . . and whenever he is ready, I will fight him with any number from one to ten thousand cavalry. . . . Gin'ral Wilson may pick his men and I'll pick mine. He may take his sabers and I'll take my six shooters. I don't want nary a saber in my command—haven't got one." When Hosea mentioned that as a graduate of West Point he believed in using sabers, Forrest replied, "I ain't no graduate of West Point, and never rubbed my back up against no college, but Wilson may take his sabers and I'll use my six shooters and agree to whip the fight with any cavalry he can bring."[48]

While Forrest tried to reconstitute his forces, the Federal forces were just biding their time. Major General Wilson had assembled 22,000 men in two large camps north of the Tennessee River. Sixteen thousand of these were well mounted and equipped and were prepared to ride against the Confederates. Forrest's scouts reported these developments, and he sent the word to Chalmers; "Spare no time, hasten to reorganize and fit up your command. We have no time to lose."[49]

General Wilson planned to attack Selma, Alabama, a major munitions and manufacturing center. It also served as a depot for two railroads, the Alabama and Tennessee Rivers Railroad that ran north to Blue Mountain and the Alabama and Mississippi Rivers Railroad that ran west toward Meridian.

Heavy spring rains delayed the movements of Wilson, who had to wait two weeks for the Tennessee River to fall. He had sent ahead one division under Maj. Gen. Edward Canby to operate against Mobile. On March 18, Wilson began crossing with three divisions that included 12,500 mounted men armed with Spencer rifles, 3 batteries, and a supply train of 250 wagons guarded by 1,500 dismounted men.[50]

On March 22, Wilson began his southward advance toward Selma. The Union force advanced in three columns over a wide area to forage along the way and to conceal its true destination. Wilson moved quickly and by the 29th had crossed the Black Warrior River. Wilson detached Brig. Gen. John Croxton and 1,100 men toward Tuscaloosa to burn anything of military value. They torched the University of Alabama and a foundry and factories. But Croxton did not rejoin Wilson during this campaign.[51]

Forrest desperately tried to delay the Union columns as they advanced. But he had not yet pulled his forces together. As Wilson encountered the small units of Forrest's men and the state troops thrown into the path of his advance, he was able to sweep them aside and continue toward Selma. On March 31, he reached Montevallo and burned ironworks, mills, and other property.[52]

At Montevallo, Wilson ran into fragments of Forrest's men hurried up to delay the Yankee cavalry. Forrest, though, arrived from Centerville just as the Federal forces had overwhelmed the small Confederate force trying to block the Union advance. Wilson wrote that Forrest was "a bold and resolute man . . . not easily rattled." Arriving with his seventy-five-man escort, he struck at the Union column just behind the advancing Union troops. Forrest managed to cleave the Union force in two, fought one half and drove it away, and then fought the other segment. Forrest temporarily stopped Wilson's advance, captured some prisoners, and escaped with many of the Confederate wounded.[53]

During the night, Wilson received word that his men had captured one of Forrest's couriers. The messages he carried revealed that the Confederates had only a small part of their force in front of him while the other portions were trying to catch up. With this news and the knowledge that high water had kept the rebels from crossing the rain-swollen Cahaba River, Wilson sent a brigade to form a junction with Croxton at Jackson and to destroy the bridge at Centerville in order to keep Forrest from merging his forces. Forrest now had only about 1,500 men, including 300 militia sent from Selma to keep Wilson's 9,000 men out of the city.[54]

At dawn on the 1st, Wilson's men mounted and rode to find and defeat the Confederates in their front. At 4 P.M., the Federal soldiers appeared, and Wilson, believing he could brush aside the Confederates, sent four companies of the Seventeenth Indiana Cavalry with sabers drawn, to ride against Forrest. As the Federal cavalry swept toward the Confederate line, Forrest ordered his men to hold their fire until they were within a hundred yards. Near a small chapel called Ebenezer Church, Forrest, with his escort and two companies, became engaged in a desperate struggle as the Indiana cavalry rode among the Confederates. It was a contest of sabers against six-shooters. During the fight, much of the action centered around Forrest. At one point, the general was surrounded by six hacking Federals. They struck blows on his head and arms, and one slash knocked the pistol from his hand. Capt. James D. Taylor singled out Forrest and succeeded with his saber in inflicting on the general his fourth wound of the war. Forrest, however, managed to kill Taylor with his pistol. Forrest claimed that if the Hoosier captain had used "the point of his saber instead of the edge, and, he had known enough to do that, I should not have been here to tell you about it."[55]

Wilson's overwhelming numbers eventually drove the Confederates from the field. Forrest, covered in blood from the saber wound, halted his men twenty-four miles south of Plantersville, having fought a running battle all the way. The Battle of Ebenezer Church had cost the Federals only about fifty casualties, but Forrest lost three artillery pieces and about three hundred men, most of whom were captured. More important, he failed to delay Wilson's march on Selma.[56]

Forrest rode into Selma early on the morning of April 2. He immediately began preparations to defend the city. He had only three thousand men, including old men and boys, to defend three and a half miles of entrenchments. The defensive works, however, were incomplete, and the artillery was left with only a small supply of ammunition and not a single charge of grape or canister.[57]

Wilson arrived outside the city on the afternoon of the 2d. He carefully reconnoitered the defenses and at 5 P.M. attacked. He sent two divisions forward, and they initially met resolute fire from the Confederate lines but broke through. Forrest tried to rally the defenders, but they could not close the gap, and the Union troops swarmed into the town. By dark Wilson held one of the most important industrial centers of the Confederacy, as well as about 2,700 prisoners, at a cost of 42 killed, about 270 wounded, and 13 missing.[58]

Forrest escaped with his escort and a number of men from other units. Just as they arrived on the outskirts of town, however, they met a small force of Union soldiers. Compelled to fight their way through these men, Forrest killed his thirtieth enemy since his first engagement, at Sacramento in 1861. He finished his combat career with only one fewer horse shot out from under him.[59]

The next day, Forrest proceeded west. In Marion he met Brig. Gen. William H. Jackson's division and part of Chalmers's. On the 8th, Forrest met with Wilson at Cahaba, Alabama, to discuss the exchange of prisoners. Forrest, with his arm still in a sling, looked haggard. Forrest told Wilson that he had no authority to exchange men but would ask his superiors. Forrest remained in this area, trying to reassemble and refit his command. After establishing this headquarters at Gainesville on the 15th, he received news of the surrender of Lee's army at Appomattox.[60]

On the 25th, rumors of Gen. Joseph Johnston's negotiations with Sherman for cessation of hostilities circulated in the ranks. Forrest tried to reassure his men by issuing an address. He asked them to "stand firm" and asked that they all continue to do their duty to "country, to yourselves, and the gallant dead who have fallen in this great struggle for liberty and independence." He assured his soldiers that in a few days he would determine the truth of the reports and asked them to "preserve untarnished the reputation you have so nobly won."[61]

Gloom and despair filled the Confederate camps. Forrest was also melancholy, not knowing what to do. For several days, he considered escaping to Mexico. On long rides with his adjutant, Charles A. Anderson, he discussed this option. One night while speaking of this topic, they came to a fork in the road. Anderson asked, "Which way, General?" Forrest answered, "Either. If one road led to hell and the other to Mexico, I would be indifferent as to which to take." Anderson pointed out that duty required the general to lead into peace the young men who had followed him during the war. Forrest thought for a moment and said, "That settles it," and he turned back to camp.[62]

Forrest returned to his headquarters to await word from his superiors. There he freed his slaves. He had promised freedom to the forty-seven who rode with him during the war. Forrest proclaimed, "These boys stayed with me, drove my teams, and better Confederates did not live." Meanwhile, General Taylor was completing negotiations with Union general Canby. As the men under Forrest began to learn of Lee and Johnston's surrender, many of them became overwhelmed with grief.[63]

On May 9, Forrest addressed his troops for the last time. He advised them of the surrender terms and added, "We are beaten is a self-evident fact, and any further resistance on our part would be justly regarded as the very height of folly and rashness." He explained that "the cause for which you have so long and so manfully struggled and for which you have braved dangers, endured privations and sufferings, and made so many sacrifices, is today hopeless." He argued that no more blood should be shed, that it was their duty to lay down their arms and to restore peace and law and order. He begged his men to "divest" themselves of feelings of "animosity, hatred, and revenge" and to "cultivate friendly feelings toward those with whom we have so long contested and heretofore so widely but honestly differed." He reminded his men that they had done their duty faithfully and that their "courage and determination as exhibited on many hard-fought fields has elicited the respect and admiration of friend and foe." He told them that he had never expected anything from them that he had not been willing to do himself. He concluded, "You have been good soldiers, you can be good citizens. Obey the laws, preserve your honor, and the Government to which you have surrendered can afford to be and will be magnanimous." When Forrest finished, most of his men "who had never flinched in battle were crying like children."[64] The warrior had become a peacemaker.

Chapter 7

"We May Differ in Color, but Not in Sentiment"

U NCERTAIN OF HIS FUTURE, Forrest remained in the Gainesville area for a couple of days assisting with the parole of his men before he boarded a train to Memphis. As the overcrowded train moved slowly toward Jackson, Mississippi, one of the cars' wheels came off the tracks, causing the train to stop. Forrest, naturally, took a leadership role and ordered the men out of the cars to help with the work ahead. Forrest directed the men, who used levers, to lift the coach back onto the track. After an unsuccessful try, one man informed the general that some of the other men had refused to leave the coach to help. Forrest sprang to the steps of the coach and shouted, "If you damned rascals don't get out of here and help get this car on the track I will throw every one of you through the windows." This was warning enough. The men hurriedly left the car, and they quickly had it back on the track. The witness who recorded the incident said about Forrest, "It seemed under all conditions he was the man for the occasion."[1]

Forrest returned home "wrecked . . . completely used up—shot all to pieces, crippled up . . . a beggar." Yet he did come out of the war as the most influential and popular man in western Tennessee. Bedford, though, just wished to return to his prewar lifestyle, but he would have an uphill journey and would encounter many obstacles. During the war, he had relinquished a 1,445-acre tract of land because he could not make the payment. He still owned his large plantation in Coahoma County, Mississippi. Forrest, a smart businessman, went into partnership with a Union officer from Minnesota and hired both freed slaves and former Union soldiers to work for him. While he attempted to reclaim his financial stability, he had to endure criticism about his wartime activities.[2]

In March 1866, Forrest had an encounter with one of the freedmen on his plantation, which ended in the latter's death. The man, Tom Edwards, had a reputation for violence, abused the livestock, and regularly beat his wife. On March 31, Forrest asked Edwards to help with a project on the plantation. Edwards refused and continued toward his quarters and here began threatening his wife. Forrest intervened on the woman's behalf, and Edwards drew a knife on the general. Forrest defended himself with a broom, but Edwards managed to wound him. Forrest then noticed an ax and grabbed it. When Edwards lunged again, Forrest struck him a fatal blow with the ax. Forrest stood trial, and the jury found him innocent, having killed Edwards in self-defense.[3]

Forrest's financial situation, though, was beginning to deteriorate. In August 1866, he had to sell 3,345 acres of his Coahoma County plantation, leaving him with virtually nothing. The following month, he tried to go into business as a cotton factor, but after several months, this also failed. He then tried his hand in fire and life insurance and later joined a project to extend the Memphis and Little Rock Railroad before the end of the year.[4]

The railroad project required travel to other states to solicit other investors. The terms of his military parole, however, would not allow the travel. He had to apply to the president for amnesty. In this letter, he told the president that when he accepted his parole he had kept his pledge to "submit to the Constitutional authority of the United States." He wrote that he realized he was "regarded in large communities at the North, with abhorrence, as a detestable monster, ruthless and swift to take life, and guilty of unpardonable crimes in connection with the capture of Fort Pillow." Forrest claimed that this was misjudged and that it pained and mortified him. Forrest would not receive his pardon until July 1868.[5]

Just as Forrest's own situation seemed uncontrollable, so was the social order in the South. Reconstruction, just beginning, was doomed to failure after casting a pall on the Southern states for a dozen years. It turned society upside down by disenfranchising whites while African Americans enjoyed unlimited political freedoms. Federal officers and agents and carpetbaggers created further problems and complicated already complex social and economic issues in the South. Federal authorities often broke or disregarded Federal laws, and corruption was unchecked. To make matters worse, rampant postwar poverty and little economic autonomy gripped the region. In the summer of 1866, confusion over the new social order spawned several racial clashes in major Southern cities. In Memphis, a conflict between recently discharged African American soldiers and Irish policemen caused a deadly riot. From this chaos was born the Ku Klux Klan.

Forrest did not become involved with politics after the war and tried to avoid this activity for personal reasons. He had no thoughts of "advancement or benefit for himself." Yet, in 1867, he could no longer stand by and observe, so he chose to join the Pale Faces, an organization pledged to protect the weak and innocent and to keep order. Many likened this organization to the Masons. The Klan, developed as a similar organization, became more popular and swept through the South. Begun by ex–Confederate officers in Pulaski, Tennessee, it was originally a secret society similar to the Pale Faces. The members founded it to promote chivalry, mercy, humanity, and patriotism.[7]

Forrest was invited to join the Klan by his former chief of artillery John Morton, who was the Grand Cyclops of the Nashville Den. Forrest's participation in the Klan was precipitated by what many saw as corrupt and harsh rule by William G. Brownlow, the Republican governor of Tennessee. The Klan served Forrest and many other Southerners to support the defense of their concept of society and their principles of honor.[8]

Forrest's notoriety earned him immediate status in the Klan. This was something that Forrest never sought. He was not interested in politics but was interested in trying to wrest political control from Brownlow and restore the autonomy of the state. Basil Duke claimed, "His sole concern seemed to be to relieve his people from the terrible and oppressive conditions under which they so grievously suffered." Duke observed that Forrest worked "with the same ardor and indifference to any personal hazard which characterized him in military service."[9]

In the early days, there were no thoughts of violence, but the hooded riders' nighttime appearances bred fear, and the organization soon spread beyond Pulaski. By 1867, the Klan had evolved into a political tool, especially successful in intimidating blacks. The organization appointed Forrest the Grand Wizard of the Klan because of his notoriety and leadership skills. Some claim that the Klan offered the position to Robert E. Lee, who declined because of his poor health. Approving the concept, Lee supposedly wrote that the organization must remain "invisible." Reportedly, when the original group met in the Maxwell House to form the Klan, the group adopted Lee's notion of an "invisible" organization and hence became known as the Invisible Empire, though no evidence exists to support this. Also apocryphal is the story of how they selected Forrest as the overall leader. During the meeting, a speaker asked for nominations. From the back of the room was shouted, "The Wizard of the Saddle, General Nathan Bedford Forrest." They elected the general, and using this term, he became the Grand Wizard of the Invisible Empire. Regardless of exactly how he gained the position, Forrest received as many as one hundred letters a day and had a secretary to answer them.[10]

The early Klan's agenda centered on organizing the disenfranchised whites of the South to effect political change. By 1868, the Klan had burgeoned, and some members tried to force change through the use of violence and intimidation against blacks, members of the Republican Union League, and Loyal League organizations. Considered carpetbaggers of the worst kind, these groups organized the blacks to vote Republican.[11]

Forrest remained interested in helping to shape the New South politically by peaceful means. Nevertheless, he was not interested in holding any political position. His leadership in the Klan was an effort to create an organized group to oppose Reconstruction and the Republicans. His interests and abilities as a leader landed him an invitation to New York as a delegate in the first Democratic National Convention after the war.[12]

Taking a train, the Tennessee and Kentucky delegates traveled together. Basil Duke was among the members, and the group attracted much attention. At one town, the train stopped short of the depot and the conductor informed Forrest that the town bully planned to remove Forrest from the train and "thrash" him. The conductor suggested that Forrest remain on the train to keep the crowd from becoming involved. Forrest, a man accustomed to adversity, was not excited and calmly remained on the train. When the train stopped at the depot, a powerful man "larger than Forrest" sprung onto the platform and into the car shouting, "Where's that d——d butcher Forrest? I want him." Forrest immediately transformed himself into a warrior, and the bully gazed upon a specter that many enemies had seen before. Forrest "bounded from his seat, his form erect and dilated, his face the color of heated bronze, and his eyes flaming, blazing." Rapidly approaching his nemesis, Forrest said, "I am Forrest. . . . What do you want?" When Forrest approached, the man ran from the coach and into the crowd with Forrest behind him, shouting for him to stop. As the man disappeared around the corner, the humor of the incident struck Forrest, and he began to laugh. The crowd joined in the laughter, and as he reboarded the train, many people pressed close to shake his hand. The train left to the cheers of the crowd.[13]

Forrest drew much notice at the convention, but he did not take a prominent speaking role. During the presidential election, however, he drew the attention of retired Union general Judson Kilpatrick, who maliciously assailed Forrest in a speech claiming he had "nailed Negroes to the fences, set fire to the fences, and burned the Negroes to death" at Fort Pillow. Forrest denounced Kilpatrick as a "blackguard, a liar, a scoundrel and poltroon." Forrest refuted Kilpatrick's claims in an open letter to the newspaper. Forrest also challenged Kilpatrick to a duel on horseback with sabers. Frightened, the Union general declined, claiming he would not do so because Forrest was not a "gentleman."[14]

The Democrats, however, lost the presidential election and seemed unable to wrest political control from the Republican-held state governments. The Klan developed in Tennessee into a tool for counterrevolution and spread to the rest of the South. The disenfranchised whites used this secret organization as an arm of the Democratic Party to intimidate and terrorize those opposed to political reform. Members of the Klan used these strong-arm tactics to disrupt the Republican Party's machinery and to frustrate the efforts of Reconstruction, with designs to restore both white supremacy and racial subordination. Unfortunately, the "mask" of the organization led to "Bogus Ku Klux" groups, who used violence to carry out their own programs and perplexed the Klan's leadership about how to deal with these pretenders.[15]

In late summer 1868, Governor Brownlow threatened to mobilize the militia to deal harshly with the Klan, whom he believed were ex-Confederates bent on overthrowing the state government. Forrest and other ex–Confederate generals traveled to Nashville to assure the legislature that there was no need for the militia. Brownlow was unconvinced and continued his effort to call up troops. Forrest spoke to the press but did not speak as a moderator. In a speech in August, he advised against "civil war or war of any kind" and he counseled African Americans to stand by their former masters, not the carpetbaggers and scalawags. Yet he said, "I do not want more war . . . nor do I want to see Negroes armed to shoot down white men." He continued,

"If they bring this war upon us, there is one thing I will tell you: that I shall not shoot any Negroes as long as I can see a white radical to shoot, for it is the radicals who will be to blame for bringing on this war."[16]

To Forrest, the Radical Republicans presented a clear threat to his vision of society. The only force that existed that could negate the Loyal Leagues was the Klan. The Loyal Leagues had grown and, in some instances, had taken up arms and formed military units. Forrest, in his position as Grand Wizard, served as the chief protector of Southern society and honor.

Forrest, while heading this secret organization, continued to seek financial security. In 1868, he bought controlling interest in what would become the Selma, Marion, and Memphis Railroad. The man who so effectively destroyed railroads during the war would now be running one. As president, he attended meetings, lobbied politicians for favors, promoted the railroad, and handled many of the day-to-day operations, administrative contractors, and purchases. Forrest's various business interests, including insurance and paving, had carried him to other states, allowing him to conduct business and promote the Klan with the intention of bringing white conservative Democrats back into power.[17]

In early 1869, political fortunes began to shift in Tennessee. Brownlow, the longtime nemesis of the Democrats, continued to press for the abolition of the Klan. In February, he gathered about 1,600 militia recruits to place nine counties under martial law. Two weeks later, however, he took the oath as a U.S. Senator, and his governorship passed to DeWitt Clinton Senter, who opened the polls to thousands of ex-Confederates. These men helped him to win the state election that August. The reenfranchised Democrats now had no need of the Ku Klux Klan as a political tool, and its value as a political organization diminished. Therefore, Forrest ordered its disbandment and the destruction of all the documents and regalia.[18]

Yet by the time Forrest gave this order, he had lost control of the organization. Imitation elements had already infiltrated the Klan. Distillers, horse thieves, and other lawbreakers were using the disguise of the Klan to carry out their own agendas. There were even blacks who wore the regalia to strike at their own race. By 1870, when Forrest was no longer the head of the organization, it had begun to take a new, unsavory and increasingly criminal course. The Klan would haunt the South and the rest of the country for generations.[19]

The depredations of the Klan soon attracted the attention of Congress, which formed a joint committee to investigate the organization. On June 27, 1871, Forrest appeared before the committee. During questioning, Forrest was evasive, feigned lapses of memory, gave contradictory testimony, and supplied no credible names associated with the organization. After the strenuous session, one of his friends asked him what he had done, and Forrest beamed and said, "I have been lying like a gentleman."[20]

Forrest returned to his Alabama railroad business and for the next three years tried to lead it into solvency. The national panic of 1873 was the financial coup de grâce for the railroad, and Forrest resigned in 1874. The railroad had cost him many unhappy moments, worries, litigation, and now financial ruin.[21]

Since the war's end, Forrest had continually supported reconciliation between the North and the South. He was involved with raising funds for Confederate memorials and in May 1875 led the Confederates in a ceremony to decorate the headstones of the Union dead in Memphis. Forrest and Gideon Pillow signed a letter, published in the local paper, that spoke of the Federals who "fought gallantly for the preservation of the government . . . which is now ours, was that of our fathers, and must be that of our children."[22]

In July a more remarkable event occurred. The Independent Order of Pole-Bearers, a forerunner of the NAACP, invited Forrest to speak at a large gathering. Forrest and several other prominent whites accepted the invitation, likely with intentions of trying to bring blacks into the fold of the Democratic Party. The man accused of being the butcher at Fort Pillow, the ex–Grand Wizard of the Klan, showed at this event his true character and his open mind to racial harmony.[23]

Forrest took the stage amid an atmosphere of "peace, joy, and union." After accepting flowers from the daughter of one of the officers of the Pole-Bearers, he delivered a harmonious and conciliatory speech. He remarked, "I came here with the jeers of some white people, who think that I am doing wrong. I believe I can exert some influence, and do much to assist the people in strengthening fraternal relations." He continued, "I want to elevate you to take positions in law offices, in stores, on farms, and wherever you are capable of going." Forrest reached out to the crowd by saying, "I came to meet you as friends, and welcome you to the white people. I want you to come nearer to us . . . We may differ in color, but not in sentiment." Forrest proclaimed that men had repeated things about him that were wrong and that could be contradicted. He claimed that he had protected blacks during battle and finished to prolonged applause after stating, "Go to work, be industrious, live honestly, and act truly, and when you are oppressed, I'll come to your relief."[24]

Yet, just when Forrest might have become an influential proponent of reconciliation, his health began to deteriorate rapidly. Forrest, who had his whole life been temperate and moral, now turned to the church. When Forrest met Reverend Raleigh White on the streets of Memphis, the preacher led Forrest in prayer in the parlor of a bank. On November 7, 1875, Forrest walked into the Court Street Cumberland Presbyterian Church and became a Christian. Forrest, who never did anything piecemeal, accepted religion passionately.[25]

Forrest had endured failing health since the war's end and suffered from chronic diarrhea. He had recently missed the reunion of his old Seventh Calvary unit. In July 1877, he traveled to Hurricane Springs to attempt to restore his health, but the man who for so many years had been the picture of health was slowly dying. His once bronze face was pale and his frame now sickly thin; he weighed barely more than one hundred pounds.[26]

His friends realized he would not likely recover from his illness and helped him onto a train back to Memphis. They took Forrest to his brother Jesse's house. There Jefferson Davis and other old friends visited. At 7:30 on October 29, 1877, Forrest died at the age of fifty-six.

The funeral procession for Forrest, which included two hundred horsemen, rifle teams, and a brass band, stretched for three miles to Elmwood Cemetery. Approximately twenty-thousand people, both white and black, came to pay their respects and bid a final farewell. Jefferson Davis was one of the pallbearers and helped place Forrest at his grave. The night they laid Forrest to rest, a storm swept through Memphis with "grey rain" and a "fierce wind." Lafcadio Hern, a reporter who covered the funeral, wrote about this storm, "The queer fancy came to me that the dead Confederate cavalrymen, rejoined by their desperate leader, were fighting ghostly battles with men who died for the Union."[27]

Epilogue

The Confederate Army had twenty-four men attain the rank of lieutenant general or higher. Twenty of these men graduated from West Point and before the war served in the U.S. Army. Another, Sterling Price, was a former governor of Missouri, fought in the Mexican War, and commanded the Missouri State forces. In June 1861, Richard Taylor, the son of General and President Zachary Taylor, was a colonel of the Ninth Louisiana, and Wade Hampton was the colonel of the Hampton Legion. When Forrest enlisted, all these men were already officers in Confederate service.[28]

The roots of Forrest's rise to greatness as a military commander go back to his childhood on the frontier. There he learned self-reliance. In this often violent society, he developed into a rough and rugged individual—necessary traits for survival and success. Forrest learned the need for direct action. He also exhibited a passionate and quick temper. Control of this temper was less essential in the mid–nineteenth century than in modern society. His outbursts among his neighbors, his adversaries, his men, and his superiors today would have destroyed his business chances and ended his military career.

Yet he possessed other traits that translated into positive military characteristics. He often found it difficult to serve as a sub-ordinate because he wanted control and disliked being a specta-tor. Forrest continually influenced his destiny by acting decisively. In battle, he always sought to be on the offensive and strove to keep the initiative. This kept his enemy off balance. He rarely stood to receive an attack. Instead, he often launched his whole command at the enemy with confidence and attacked with persistence in order to shock the enemy and "overawe and demoralize them." Forrest's contemporaries considered him the "negative of the West Pointer," because he had "no preconceived ideas of military science" and held in contempt the idea that only those who graduated from West Point could command. He once said, "Whenever I met one of them fellers that fit by note, I generally whipped h——ll out of him before he got his tune pitched."[29]

Forrest's aggressiveness was only one of his traits. He was al-ways in advance, to observe personally the terrain and the enemy in order to deploy his men effectively. He showed a keen under-standing of the use of artillery. His instinctive use of flank at-tacks successfully and repeatedly demoralized his enemies. He often used the cover of woods to make this even more effective. Additionally, his "fierce and untimely pursuit" often altered a de-feat of his enemy into a rout. He had a good eye for position and either picked favorable ground for a fight or could find a weak-ness in his enemy's position. His forces actively raided, screened, scouted, and fought. He was a true combat leader, had good in-stincts, and showed personal courage and boldness while being unshakable on the field of battle. General Richard Taylor ex-plained his ferocity in a fight. He doubted "if any commander since the days of lion-hearted Richard has killed as many ene-mies with his own hand as Forrest." Forrest knew well that "war means fighting and fighting means killing."[30]

Forrest constantly created difficult situations for his Union adversaries. He never had more than fifteen thousand men un-der his command. Yet his presence in the field cost the Union vast resources of men, animals, and supplies to defeat or to neutralize him. His success came, in part, because he effectively used horses to transport his men rapidly on the field of battle. His forces resembled the seventeenth-century dragoons who rode as mounted infantry, but they became the model for twentieth-century mechanized infantry. General Chalmers claimed they were "winged infantry." Forrest, despite the disadvantage of small numbers, strategically changed the center of gravity in the Western Theatre during most of the war.[31]

Many have pondered his ability to successfully handle higher command. While we will never know if he could lead successfully larger bodies of men, he was capable of making quick decisions and remained calm and reasonable in time of crisis. He was also a natural leader and rarely wasted men in fruitless encounters. His keen understanding of position and logistics was essential. Furthermore, Forrest always worked best in semi-independent commands.

Forrest's contemporaries thought highly of him. Reportedly, someone asked Robert E. Lee to name the greatest soldier produced on either side during the war, and he replied, "A man I have never seen, sir. His name is Forrest." General Sherman also had a high opinion of Forrest and said, "Forrest was the most remarkable man our Civil War produced on either side."[32]

Forrest will always have his detractors. His links with the Fort Pillow controversy and the Invisible Empire and his ardent defense of his personal vision of honor and Southern society are difficult to put into perspective in a brief biography. Historians who have closely scrutinized Forrest, however, have absolved him of villainy. In 1905, Forrest and his wife were re-interred under a statute of the general on horseback in a park named for him. Forrest would rest in peace for just over eighty years. In 1988, the NAACP asked for the removal of the statue and Forrest and his wife to a less prominent place. The man who stirred such controversy in life continues to do so in death.

Notes

Chapter 1

1. In 1843, Mariam Forrest married Joseph Luxton and bore more children—three sons and a daughter. The material in this chapter comes from John Allan Wyeth's *That Devil Forrest: Life of General Nathan Bedford Forrest* (Baton Rouge: Louisiana State University Press, 1989) 1–20; Thomas Jordan and J. P. Pryor, *The Campaigns of Lieut.-Gen. N. B. Forrest and of Forrest's Cavalry* (New York: Da Capo Press, 1996) 17–35; Robert Selph Henry, *"First With the Most" Forrest*, (New York: Mallard Press, 1991) 13–31; J. Harvey Mathes, *General Forrest* (New York: D. Appleton and Company, 1902) 1–22; Ozias Midwinter [Lafcadio Hern], "Notes on Forrest's Funeral," *The Cincinnati Commercial*, November 6, 1877; and Annah Robinson Watson, "The Boyhood of Nathan Bedford Forrest," *The Commercial Appeal* (Memphis), May 14, 1905.

2. Wyeth, *That Devil Forrest*, 554.

3. *The Phenix*, March 15, 1845.

4. J. H. Curtis, "Negro Woman, Slave Sold by Forrest, Recalls Days of Old," *The Commercial Appeal* (Memphis), April 28, 1933.

Chapter 2

1. Jordan and Pryor, *Forrest*, 40.

2. Henry, *First With The Most*, 31; Wyeth, *That Devil Forrest*, 21.

3. Charles W. Button, "Early Engagements With Forrest," *Confederate Veteran* 9 (September 1897), 478; Wyeth, *That Devil Forrest*, 21; Henry, *First With The Most*, 32.

4. Henry, *First With The Most*, 34; Jordan and Pryor, *Forrest*, 42–43.

5. Samuel Tate to Sidney Johnston, November 4, 1861, eds. R. N. Scott et al., *The War of the Rebellion: A Compilation of the Official Records of the Union and Confederate Armies*. 70 vols. (Washington, D.C.: Government Printing Office, 1880–1901), ser. 1, 4:513 hereinafter cited as ORA; Wyeth, *That Devil Forrest*, 24.

6. Button, "Early Engagements With Forrest," 478–79; Jordan and Pryor, *Forrest*, 44–45.

7. There is no information concerning the loss of this vessel in the ORA. It was likely a speculative cargo to be sold to the U.S. Army. Ibid.

8. The *Conestoga* had no orders to seize clothing. She was merely on patrol. Jordan and Pryor, *Forrest*, 45; Phelps to Foote, November 19, 1861, eds. Richard Rush et al., *Official Records of the Union and Confederate Navies in the War of the Rebellion*, 31 vols. (Washington, D.C.: Government Printing Office, 1894–1927), ser. 1, 22:435–36.

9. Jordan and Pryor, *Forrest*, 47–50.

10. Report of Forrest, 30 December 1861, *ORA*, ser. 1, 7:65–66.

11. Ibid., as cited in Wyeth, *That Devil Forrest*, 30.

12. Jordan and Pryor, *Forrest*, 62–63; Wyeth, *That Devil Forrest*, 40.

13. Report of Forrest, February 1862, *ORA*, ser. 1, 7:385.

14. Ibid.; Henry, *First With The Most*, 54–55.

15. Report of Forrest, February 1862 *ORA*, ser. 1, 7, 385.

16. Jordan and Pryor, *Forrest*, 102–04; Forrest to Confederate House of Representatives, (n.d.), *ORA*, ser. 1, 7:429–31.

17. Ibid., Forrest to Confederate House of Representatives, (n.d.), *ORA*, ser. 1, 7:429–31.

18. Forrest to Confederate House of Representatives, (n.d.), *ORA*, ser. 1, 7:431.

19. Robert Selph Henry, *As They Saw Forrest: Some Recollections and Comments of Contemporaries*, (Jackson, Tenn.: McCowat-Mercer Press, 1956), IX–X.

20. Henry, *First With the Most*, 77.

21. Jordan and Pryor, *Forrest*, 127–28.

22. Ibid., 137; Wyeth, *That Devil Forrest*, 63–64; James R. Chalmers, "Forrest and His Campaigns," *Southern Historical Society Papers*, Vol. 7, No. 10 (Oct. 1899) 458.

23. Jordan and Pryor, *Forrest*, 139.

24. Ibid., 139–45.

25. Ibid., 145–46.

26. Ibid., 146–48; Henry, *First With the Most*, 81; Sherman to Grant, April 8, 1862, *ORA*, ser. 1, 7:640; Mathes, *General Forrest*, 60.

27. Jordan and Pryor, *Forrest*, 148–49.

28. Ibid., 158–59; Henry, *First With the Most*, 82.

29. Forrest to D. C. Trader, May 23, 1862, as cited in Henry, *As They Saw Forrest*, 287–88.

30. Jordan and Pryor, *Forrest*, 161, 162n.

31. Wyeth, *That Devil Forrest*, 70–72; Forrest to H. L. Clay, (n.d.) 1862, *ORA*, ser. 1, vol. 16, pt. 1, 810.

32. Forrest to Clay, ibid.; William Diffield to James B. Fry, July 23, 1862, ibid.; Jordan and Pryor, *Forrest*, 164.

33. Jordan and Pryor, *Forrest*, 164–65.

34. Forrest to Parkhurst, July 13, 1862, ibid., 805; Forrest to Clay, n.d. 1862, *ORA*, ser. 1, vol. 16, pt. 1, 810; Richard Taylor, *Destruction and Reconstruction: Personal Experiences of the Late War*, Richard B. Harwell (ed.) New York: Longmans, Green and Co., 1955, 244.

35. Forrest to Clay, ibid., 811; Basil W. Duke, *Reminiscences of General Basil W. Duke, CSA,* (Garden City, N.Y.: Doubleday, Page and Co., 1911), 346.

36. Jordan and Pryor, *Forrest*, 174–75; Wyeth, *That Devil Forrest*, 83.

37. Ibid., 176–178; Forrest to Clay, *ORA*, ser. 1, vol. 16, pt. 1, 818–19.

38. Nelson to Buell, 24, July 30, 1862, *ORA*, ser. 1, vol. 16, pt. 2, 208–09, 234; Buell to Halleck, July 26, 1862, ibid., pt. 1, 820; Nelson to Buell, July 24, 1862, ibid., 816.

Chapter 3

1. Jordan and Pryor, *Forrest*, 184, 186; G. G. Dibrell to J. P. Strange, January 6, 1863, *ORA*, ser. 1, vol. 17, pt. 1, 598.

2. Mathes, *General Forrest*, 383.

3. Forrest to Bragg, December 24, 1862, *ORA*, ser. 1, vol. 17, pt. 1, 593.

4. Sullivan to Grant, December 18, 1862, *ORA*, ser. 1, vol. 17, pt. 1, 551; Brian Steel Wills, *A Battle from the Start: The Life of Nathan Bedford Forrest* (New York: HarperCollins, 1992), 87; Henry, *As They Saw Forrest*, 110–11.

5. Forrest to Bragg, December 24, 1862, *ORA*, ser. 1, vol. 17, pt. 1, 593; Fry to Harris, January 17, 1863, ibid., 560–62; "Forrest's

West Tennessee Expedition," *The Memphis Daily Appeal,* January 27, 1863.

6. Forrest to Bragg, ibid., 594; Sullivan to Grant, ibid., pt. 2, 505.

7. Forrest to Brent, January 3, 1863, *ORA,* ser. 1, vol. 17, pt. 1, 595.

8. Ibid., 596.

9. Henry, *As They Saw Forrest,* 118; Wills, *A Battle from the Start,* 97.

10. Jordan and Pryor, *Forrest,* 221; Chalmers, "Forrest and His Campaigns," 460.

11. Ibid., *Forrest,* 225–26; Wyeth, *That Devil Forrest,* 127–28.

12. Jordan and Pryor, *Forrest,* 227–28; Wyeth, *That Devil Forrest,* 129.

13. Wheeler to Brent, February (n.d.) 1863, *ORA,* ser. 1, vol. 40, pt. 1, 40–41.

14. As quoted in Wyeth, *That Devil Forrest,* 131–32.

15. Jordan and Pryor, *Forrest,* 231–38; Forrest to [Van Dorn] March (n.d.) [1863], *ORA,* ser. 1, vol. 23, pt. 1, 120–21; Morton, *The Artillery of Nathan Bedford Forrest,* 82; Wyeth, *That Devil Forrest,* 135–43.

16. Jordan and Pryor, *Forrest,* 239–40; Wyeth, *That Devil Forrest,* 146.

17. Wyeth, *That Devil Forrest,* 150–51.

18. Ibid., 156–57; Dabney Herndon Maury, *Recollections of a Virginian in the Mexican, Indian, and Civil Wars* (New York: Charles Scribner's Sons, 1894) 207.

19. Maury, ibid., 216.

20. Streight to Whipple, August 22, 1864, *ORA,* ser. 1, vol. 23, pt. 1, 286.

21. Jordan and Pryor, *Forrest,* 249–53.

22. Ibid., 254–55; Wyeth, *That Devil Forrest,* 173.

23. Wyeth, *That Devil Forrest,* 173–74.

24. Ibid., 175.

25. Ibid., 175–76.

26. Jordan and Pryor, *Forrest,* 257–58.

27. Henry, *As They Saw Forrest,* 93.

28. Jordan and Pryor, *Forrest,* 258–59; Wyeth, *That Devil Forrest,* 178.

29. Edward G. Longacre, "All Is Fair in Love and War," *Civil War Times Illustrated,* June 1969, 37–38; Jordan and Pryor, *Forrest,* 260; as quoted in Wills, *A Battle from the Start,* 113.

30. Streight to Whipple, December 10, 1864, *ORA*, ser. 1, vol. 23, pt. 1, 289–90.

31. Wyeth, *That Devil Forrest*, 183–84.

32. Ibid., 184–85.

33. Jordan and Pryor, *Forrest*, 265.

34. Ibid., 266–67.

35. Ibid., 267–69; Wyeth, *That Devil Forrest*, 188–89.

36. Streight to Whipple, December 10, 1864, *ORA*, ser. 1, vol. 23, pt. 1, 291.

37. Ibid., 292.

38. Jordan and Pryor, *Forrest*, 273.

39. Maury, *Recollections of a Virginian*, 209.

40. Ibid.

41. Wyeth, *That Devil Forrest*, 199.

42. Morton, *The Artillery of Nathan Bedford Forrest's Cavalry*, 101.

43. Ibid., 102; Frank H. Smith, "The Forrest-Gould Affair," *Civil War Times Illustrated* (November 1970): 32; *Nashville Banner*, April 29, 1911.

44. Morton, *Forrest's Cavalry*, 102–03.

45. Ibid., 103.

46. Ibid., 104.

Chapter 4

1. Forrest to Cooper, August 9, 1863, *ORA*, ser. 1, vol. 30, pt. 4, 508–09.

2. Only five arrived before the battle.

3. Wills, *A Battle from the Start*, 133–34.

4. Henry, *First With the Most*, 182–83; Wyeth, *That Devil Forrest*, 226–27.

5. Ibid., 601; Forrest to Polk, September 21, 1863, *ORA*, ser. 1, vol. 30, pt. 4, 681.

6. Henry, *First With the Most*, 193.

7. Wyeth, *That Devil Forrest*, 241–42.

8. Ibid., 242–43.

9. Ibid., 243–44; Wills, *A Battle from the Start*, 147.

10. Jordan and Pryor, *Forrest*, 357–58, 363.

11. Forrest to Johnston, December 6, 1863, *ORA*, ser. 1, vol. 31, pt. 3, 789.

12. Jordan and Pryor, *Forrest*, 365; Wyeth, *That Devil Forrest*, 257–58.

13. Wyeth, *That Devil Forrest*, 258–59; Jordan and Pryor, *Forrest*, 378.

14. Wyeth, *That Devil Forrest*, 261–62.

15. Henry, *First With the Most*, 209.

16. Wyeth, *That Devil Forrest*, 263–64; Jordan and Pryor, *Forrest*, 378–79.

17. Forrest General Order No. 1, January 26, 1864, *ORA*, ser. 1, vol. 32, pt. 2, 617; Jordan and Pryor, *Forrest*, 383.

18. Henry, *First With the Most*, 222–34.

19. Wyeth, *That Devil Forrest*, 278–79.

20. Forrest to Jack, March 8, 1864, *ORA*, ser, 1, vol. 32, pt. 1, 350–53.

21. John P. Young, *The Seventh Tennessee Cavalry*, Nashville, 1890, 77.

22. Jordan and Pryor, *Forrest*, 395–96, Wyeth, *That Devil Forrest*, 291.

23. Ibid., 292; Jordan and Pryor, *Forrest*, 398.

24. Jordan and Pryor, *Forrest*, 399–400.

25. Forrest to Jack, March 8, 1864, *ORA*, ser. 1, vol. 32, pt. 1, 355; Wyeth, *That Devil Forrest*, 295.

26. U. S. Grant, *Personal Memoir of U. S. Grant*, 2 vols., (New York: Charles L. Webster & Company, 1885), 2:108–09.

27. Wyeth, *That Devil Forrest*, 300–01; Forrest to Jack, March 21, 1864, *ORA*, ser. 1, vol. 32, pt. 3, 664–65; Strange to Reed, ibid., 118.

28. Henry, *First With the Most*, 239; Wyeth, *That Devil Forrest*, 303.

29. Forrest to Hicks, March 25, 1864, *ORA*, ser. 1, vol. 32, pt. 1, 547.

30. Wyeth, *That Devil Forrest*, 305.

31. Forrest to Jack, April 4, 1864, *ORA*, ser. 1, vol. 32, pt. 1, 608–09.

32. Henry, *First With the Most*, 249; Albert Castel, "The Fort Pillow Massacre: A Fresh Examination of the Evidence," 38–39.

33. John Cimprich and Robert C. Mainfort Jr., "The Fort Pillow Massacre: A Statistical Note," *The Journal of American History*, vol. 76, No. 3, December 1989, 836.

34. Wyeth, *That Devil Forrest*, 314; Henry, *First With the Most*, 250.

35. Henry, ibid.

36. Jordan and Pryor, *Forrest*, 439; Wyeth, *That Devil Forrest*, 317.

37. Jordan and Pryor, *Forrest*, 429–30; Wyeth, *That Devil Forrest*, 317–18.

38. Forrest to Booth, April 12, 1864, *ORA*, ser. 1, vol. 32, pt. 1, 596.

39. Jordan and Pryor, *Forrest*, 431n.

40. Forrest to Booth, April 12, 1864, *ORA*, ser. 2, vol. 32, pt. 1, 561.

41. Charles W. Anderson, "The True Story of Fort Pillow," *Confederate Veteran*, Vol. III, No. II, November 1895: 322–23.

42. Jordan and Pryor, *Forrest*, 435; Booth to Forrest, April 12, 1864, *ORA*, ser. 1, vol. 32, pt. 1, 561.

43. Wyeth, *That Devil Forrest*, 324–25.

44. Weaver to Smith, April 22, 1864, *ORA*, ser. 1, vol. 32, pt. 1, 539.

45. Ibid.; Henry, *First With the Most*, 256.

46. Anderson, "The True Story of Fort Pillow," 324; *Report of the Committee on the Conduct of War: Fort Pillow Massacre*, 38th Cong., 1st sess., Report No. 65, Washington, D.C.: GPO, 1864, 86.

47. Lamberg to Kappner, April 20, 1864, *ORA*, ser. 1, vol. 32, pt. 1, 566.

48. Wyeth, *That Devil Forrest*, 229–30.

49. Conduct of War, 1–7, passim.

50. Henry, *First With the Most*, 248–49.

51. C. Fitch, "Capture of Fort Pillow—Vindication of General Chalmers by a Federal Officer," Southern Historical Society Papers, Vol. 7, No. 9 (Sept. 1879) 439–41.

52. Forrest to Jack, April 15, 1864, *ORA*, ser. 1, vol. 32, pt. 1, 610; Forrest to Washburn, June 23, 1864, ibid., 591.

Chapter 5

1. Jordan and Pryor, *Forrest*, 454–55; Forrest to Jack, April 15, 1864, *ORA*, ser. 1, vol. 32, pt. 1, 610.

2. Henry, *First With the Most*, 271; Forrest to Davis, April 15, 1864, *ORA*, ser. 1, vol. 32, pt. 1, 611–13; Davis to Forrest, June 9, 1864, *ORA*, ser. 1, vol. 52, pt. 2, 675–76.

3. Sherman to Rawlins, April 19, 1864, *ORA*, ser. 1, vol. 32, pt. 3, 411.

4. Henry, *First With the Most*, 282–83; Washburn to Clark, 20 July 1864, *ORA*, ser. 1, vol. 39, pt. 1, 86.

5. Henry, *First With the Most*, 283–84.

6. Edwin C. Bearss, *Forrest at Brice's Cross Roads* (Dayton, Ohio: Morningside Bookshop, 1979), 62–65.

7. Wyeth, *That Devil Forrest*, 351–52.

8. Ibid.

9. Jordan and Pryor, *Forrest*, 469; Wyeth, *That Devil Forrest*, 353; Henry, *First With the Most*, 289; Waring to Woodward, June 17, 1864, *ORA*, ser. 1, vol. 39, pt. 1, 132.

10. Henry, ibid.

11. Grierson to Rawolle, 221 June 1864, *ORA*, ser. 1, vol. 39, pt. 1, 129; Sturgis to Morgan, June 24, 1864, ibid., 92.

12. Bearss, *Brice's Cross Roads*, 71, 77.

13. Henry, *As They Saw Forrest*, 238

14. Henry, *First With the Most*, 291–92; John Milton Hubbard, *Notes of a Private* (Memphis, Tenn.: H.E. Clark & Brother, 1909), 99.

15. Wyeth, *That Devil Forrest*, 362.

16. Ibid.

17. Ibid., 363.

18. Morton, *The Artillery of Nathan Bedford Forest*, 178–79.

19. Henry, *First With the Most*, 293; Sturgis to Morgan, June 24, 1864, *ORA*, ser. 1, vol. 39, pt. 1, 93.

20. Proceedings of a Board of Investigation, ibid., 155, 213–14.

21. Ibid., 178, 180; Henry, *First With the Most*, 294, Henry, *As They Saw Forrest*, 240–41.

22. Proceedings of a Board of Investigation, *ORA*, ser. 1, vol. 39, pt. 1, 171.

23. Henry, *First With the Most*, 300.

24. Sherman to Stanton, June 14, 1864, *ORA*, ser. 1, vol. 38, pt. 4, 474; Sherman to Stanton, June 15, 1864, ibid., vol. 39, pt. 2, 121.

25. Sherman to McPherson, June 16, 1864, *ORA*, ser. 1, vol. 39, pt. 2, 123.

26. Smith to Morgan, August 5, 1864, *ORA*, ser. 1, vol. 39, pt. 1, 250; Jordan and Pryor, *Forrest*, 498; Morton, *The Artillery of Nathan Bedford Forrest*, 203.

27. Henry, *First With the Most*, 314; Jordan and Pryor, *Forrest*, 498; Forrest to Ellis, August 1, 1864, *ORA*, ser. 1, vol. 39, pt. 1, 320; Chalmers to Anderson, 23 July 1864, ibid., 325.

28. Jordan and Pryor, *Forrest*, 499–501; Henry, *First With the Most*, 315.

29. Morton, *Artillery of Nathan Bedford Forrest*, 204–05.

30. Forrest to Ellis, August 1, 1864, *ORA*, ser. 1, vol. 39, pt. 1, 322; Jordan and Pryor, *Forrest*, 501; Bearss, *Brice's Cross Roads*, 199.

31. Bearss, *Brice's Cross Roads*, 201, 351–52; Jordan and Pryor, *Forrest*, 508–09; Forrest to Ellis, August 1, 1864, *ORA*, ser. 1, vol. 39, pt.

1, 322; Smith to Morgan, August 5, 1864, *ORA*, ser. 1, vol. 39, pt. 1, 252.

32. As quoted in Henry, *First With the Most*, 323.

33. Forrest to Ellis, August 1, 1864, *ORA*, ser. 1, vol. 39, pt. 1, 323; Smith to Morgan, August 5, 1864, ibid., 253.

34. Wyeth, *That Devil Forrest*, 398; Sherman to Washburn, August 7, 1864, *ORA*, ser. 1, vol. 39, pt. 2, 233.

35. Washburn to Sherman, 23, 25 July 1864, *ORA*, ser. 1, vol. 39, pt. 2, 201, 204.

36. Goodhue to McCallum, 28 July 1864, ibid., 208; Henry, *First With the Most*, 328–29.

37. Maury to Forrest, August 2, 1864, *ORA*, ibid., 748.

38. Bearss, *Brice's Cross Roads*, 268–69.

39. There was a skirmish on the 13th. Jordan and Pryor, *Forrest*, 534–35; Henry, *That Devil Forrest*, 333–34.

40. Henry, *First With the Most*, 334–35.

41. Wyeth, *That Devil Forrest*, 412–13.

42. Jordan and Pryor, *Forrest*, 539–41.

43. Henry, *First With the Most*, 338.

44. Ibid., 339; Jordan and Pryor, *Forrest*, 544–45.

45. Jordan and Pryor, *Forrest*, 545–46; Maury, *Recollections of a Virginian*, 215.

46. Washburn to Clark, September 2, 1864, *ORA*, ser. 1, vol. 39, pt. 1, 469.

Chapter 6

1. Taylor, *Destruction and Reconstruction*, 242.

2. Ibid., 242–43.

3. Henry, *First With the Most*, 350.

4. Strange to Ellis, September 16, 1864, *ORA*, ser. 1, vol. 39, pt. 2, 839–40; Jordan and Pryor, *Forrest*, 558–59.

5. Forrest to Ellis, October 17, 1864, *ORA*, ser. 1, vol. 39, pt. 1, 542–43.

6. Jordan and Pryor, *Forrest*, 562–63.

7. Ibid., 564; Forrest to Ellis, October 17, 1864, *ORA*, ser. 1, vol. 39, pt. 1, 543–44; March to Willett, December 2, 1864, ibid., 519.

8. Morton, *Forrest*, 231–32.

9. Ibid., 232; Henry, *First With the Most*, 355.

10. Jordan and Pryor, *Forrest*, 566–568.

11. Ibid., 568–570; Granger to Polk, October 10, 1864, *ORA*, ser. 1, vol. 39, pt. 1, 514.

12. Jordan and Pryor, *Forrest*, 570.

13. Forrest to Ellis, October 17, 1864, *ORA*, ser. 1, vol. 39, pt. 1, 545; Jordan and Pryor, *Forrest*, 572–73.

14. Forrest to Ellis, ibid., 546.

15. Ibid., 546–48.

16. Henry, *First With the Most*, 363.

17. Ibid., 365; Forrest to Taylor, October 8, 1864, *ORA*, ser. 1, vol. 39, pt. 3, 807.

18. Forrest to Taylor, October 12, 1864, ibid., 815–16; Forrest to Chalmers, ibid., 817; Wyeth, *That Devil Forrest*, 456.

19. "Capture of the *Mazeppa*," *Confederate Veteran*, December 1905, vol. XIII. no. 12, 566–70; Forrest to Surget, January 12, 1865, *ORA*, ser. 1, vol. 39, pt. 1, 870.

20. Morton, *The Artillery of Nathan Bedford Forrest's Calvary*, 247–48.

21. Statement of Acting Master J. L. Bryant (n.d.), *ORN*, ser. 1, vol. 26, 602–03.

22. Ibid.

23. Jordan and Pryor, *Forrest*, 596–97.

24. Ibid., 598.

25. Forrest to Surget, January 12, 1864, *ORA*, ser. 1, vol. 39, pt. 1, 870–71.

26. Henry, *First With the Most*, 375–76.

27. Ibid., 377; Forrest to Surget, January 12, 1864, *ORA*, ser. 1, vol. 39, pt. 1, 871.

28. Forrest to Surget, ibid; Sinclair to Hardie, January 7, 1865, *ORA*, ser. 1, vol. 39, pt. 1, 862.

29. Fithian to Hooker, November 7, 1864, *ORA*, ser. 1, vol. 39, pt. 3, 694; Sherman to Grant, November 6, 1864, ibid., 659; William T. Sherman, *Memoirs of General William T. Sherman*. 2 vols. (New York: D. Appleton and Company, 1875), 2:164.

30. Jordan and Pryor, 611–12; Forrest to Mason, January 24, 1865, *ORA*, ser. 1, vol. 45, pt. 1, 752.

31. Henry, *First With the Most*, 385.

32. Forrest to Mason, January 24, 1865, *ORA*, ser. 1, vol. 45, pt. 1, 752.

33. Ibid.; J. P. Young, "Hood's Failure at Spring Hill," *Confederate Veteran*, vol. XVI, no. 1 (January 1908), 31.

34. Forrest to Mason, January 24, 1865, *ORA*, ser. 1, vol. 45, pt. 1, 753.

35. Ibid.

36. Henry, *First With the Most*, 402–03.

37. Ibid., 403; Forrest to Mason, January 24, 1865, *ORN*, ser. 1, vol. 45, pt. 1, 755.

38. Morton, *The Artillery of Nathan Bedford Forrest's Calvary*, 282–84.

39. Forrest to Mason, January 24, 1865, *ORA*, ser. 1, vol. 45, pt. 1, 756.

40. Ibid., 756–57; quoted in Christopher Losson, *Tennessee's Forgotten Warriors: Frank Cheatham and His Confederate Division* (Knoxville: The University of Tennessee Press, 1989), 240.

41. Forrest to Mason, January 24, 1865, *ORA*, ser. 1, vol. 45, pt. 1, 757.

42. Ibid.; Jordan and Pryor, *Forrest*, 648–49.

43. Ibid., 650–51.

44. Ibid., 651–52; Forrest to Mason, January 24, 1865, *ORA*, ser. 1, vol. 45, pt. 1, 758.

45. Pryor to Jordan, ibid., 652–53; Forrest to Mason, ibid.

46. Jordan and Pryor, *Forrest*, 655–56; address of Maj. Gen. N. B. Forrest to his troops (n.d.), *ORA*, ser. 1, vol. 45, pt. 1, 759–60.

47. Jordan and Pryor, *Forrest*, 656–58.

48. Lewis M. Hosea to his sister, February 26, 1865, Monroe Fulkerson Cockrell Papers, Special Collections, Perkins Library, Duke University, Durham, N.C.

49. Ibid., 658; Forrest to Chalmers, February 19, 1865, *ORA*, ser. 1, vol. 49, pt. 1, 994.

50. Wilson to Whipple, June 29, 1865, *ORA*, ser. 1, vol. 49, pt. 1, 355; Henry, *First With the Most*, 427.

51. Wilson to Whipple, ibid., 356–57; Croxton to Bacon, May (n.d.) 1865, ibid., 420–21.

52. Itinerary of the Cavalry Corps, Military Division of the Mississippi (n.d.), ibid., 383–84.

53. Henry, *First With the Most*, 430; Wyeth claims that Forrest also had two hundred men from Gen. Frank Armstrong; James Harrison Wilson, *Under the Old Flag*, 2 vols. (New York: D. Appleton and Company, 1912), 2:208.

54. Henry, ibid.; Wilson to McCook, *ORA*, ser. 1, vol. 49, pt. 2, 173.

55. Wyeth, *That Devil Forrest*, 531–32; Henry, *First With the Most*, 430–31; Wilson, *Under the Old Flag*, 2: 217, 244.

56. Wills, *A Battle from the Start,* 309.

57. Henry, *First With the Most,* 431–32; Jordan and Pryor, *Forrest,* 637.

58. Minty to Beaumont, May 10, 1865, *ORA,* ser. 1, vol. 49, pt. 1, 444.

59. Wyeth, *That Devil Forrest,* 536.

60. Jordan and Pryor, *Forrest,* 678–79; Henry, *First With the Most,* 436; Wilson, *Under the Old Flag,* 2: 240–45.

61. Address of Forrest, April 25, 1865, *ORA,* ser. 1, vol. 49, pt. 2, 1263–64.

62. "Group of Officers of Forrest's Cavalry." *Confederate Veteran,* April 1908, vol. XVI, no. 4, xxvi; Henry, *First With the Most,* 437.

63. *Cincinnati Commercial,* August 28, 1868; "George W. Cable's Recollections of General Forrest," Arlin Turner (ed.), *The Journal of Southern History,* vol. 21, no. 2, May 1955, 228.

64. J. G. Witherspoon, "General Forrest's Military Strategy," *Confederate Veteran,* vol. XXIII, no. 7, July 1955, 318; Address of Forrest, May 9, 1865, *ORA,* ser. 1, vol. 49, pt. 2, 1289–90.

Chapter 7

1. Wyeth, *That Devil Forrest,* 545–46.

2. Forrest Testimony, *Ku Klux Conspiracy: Report of the Joint Select Committee to Inquire into the Condition of Affairs in the Late Insurrectionary States,* 42nd Cong., 2nd sess., Sen. Rpt. No. 41, Vol. 13, 24; Henry, *First With the Most,* 440–41; Wills, *A Battle from the Start,* 320–25.

3. Wills, *A Battle from the Start,* 325–30.

4. Jack Hurst, *Nathan Bedford Forrest: A Biography* (New York: Alfred A. Knopf, 1993), 280–82.

5. Ibid., 282; Forrest to Johnston, November 25, 1866, N.B. Forrest Papers Special Collections, Duke University.

6. Basil W. Duke, *Reminiscences of General Basil W. Duke, CSA,* (Garden City, N.Y.: Doubleday, Page and Co., 1911), 346.

7. Wills, *A Battle from the Start,* 334; Stanley F. Horn, *Invisible Empire: The Story of the Ku Klux Klan 1866–1871* (New York: Haskell House, 1973), 1.

8. Morton, *The Artillery of Nathan Bedford Forest,* 344–45.

9. Duke, *Reminiscences,* 346.

10. Andrew Nelson Lytle, *Bedford Forrest and His Critter Company* (Nashville, TN: J. S. Sanders, Co., 1996), 383; Henry, *First With the Most,* 447–48; Horn, *Invisible Empire,* 17–20.

11. Wyn Craig Wade, *The Fiery Cross: The Ku Klux Klan in America* (New York: Oxford University Press), 1998.
12. Duke, *Reminiscences*, 348.
13. Ibid., 348–49.
14. Ibid., 350–55; Henry, *First With the Most*, 454–55; Samuel J. Martin, *Kill-Cavalry: The Life of Union General Hugh Judson Kilpatrick* (Mechanicsburg, PA: Stackpole Books, 2000), 246.
15. Eric Foner, *Reconstruction: America's Unfinished Revolution 1863–1877* (New York: Harper & Row, 1988), 425–26; Horn, *Invisible Empire*, 363–64.
16. As cited in Hurst, *Forrest*, 307–11.
17. Wills, *A Battle from the Start*, 356–57.
18. Hurst, *Forrest*, 326–27.
19. Horn, *Invisible Empire*, 367–68, 372; Wade, *The Fiery Cross*, 59.
20. U.S. Congress, *Ku Klux Conspiracy: Report of the Joint Select Committee to Inquire into the Condition of Affairs in the Late Insurrectionary States*, 42nd Cong., 2nd sess., Sen. Rpt. No. 41, vol. 31, 3–32; Horn, *Invisible Empire*, 316.
21. Henry, *First With the Most*, 457–58.
22. Hurst, *Forrest*, 364–65.
23. Ibid., 366.
24. Ibid., 366–67.
25. Henry, *First With the Most*, 459–60.
26. Ibid., 460.
27. Ibid., 461–62; Ozias Midwinter, [Lafcadio Hern] "Notes on Forrest's Funeral," *The Cincinnati Commercial*, November 6, 1877.
28. Henry, *First With the Most*, 471n.
29. Morton, *The Artillery of Nathan Bedford Forest*, p 12–13; Theodore Goodloe Albert, *Confederate Echoes* (Nashville, TN: By the author, 1983), 179; Chalmers, "Forrest and His Campaigns," 454.
30. Taylor, *Destruction and Reconstruction*, 244; Wyeth, *That Devil Forrest*, 370.
31. Chalmers, "Forrest and His Campaigns," 455, 457.
32. Lytle, *Bedford Forrest and His Critter Company*, 357; Henry, *First With the Most*, 471; Wyeth, *That Devil Forrest*, 561.

Bibliographic Note

Forrest attracted biographers within a few years after the war. The first biography was written by Thomas Jordan and John P. Pryor. In 1868, they published *The Campaigns of Lieut.-Gen. N. B. Forrest, and of Forrest's Cavalry* (New Orleans: Blelock & Co.). Jordan and Pryor were Memphis journalists and ex–Confederate officers. They used Forrest's private papers, interviewed him, and allowed Forrest to review the manuscript. This is the closest work to an autobiography that exists. Forrest died before he could provide further information to other historians. While Jordan and Pryor's book is a valuable source of information, it is somewhat biased. The next book appeared in 1899, written by a physician, John Allan Wyeth. Entitled *Life of General Nathan Bedford Forrest* (New York: Harper & Bros.), Wyeth did much research and wrote an accurate and analytical biography that still stands as solid work. J. Harvey Mathes followed this a few years later with *General Forrest* (New York: D. Appleton & Co., 1902). Mathes was able to provide details of Forrest's early life that had never been told.

Other biographies such as Eric William Sheppard's *Bedford Forrest: The Confederacy's Greatest Cavalryman* (New York: Dial Press, 1930) and Andrew Nelson Lytle's *Bedford Forrest and His Critter Company* (New York: G. P. Putnam's Sons, 1931) are less useful. In 1944, Robert Selph Henry published *"First With the Most"* (Indianapolis: Bobbs-Merrill Co.). With the advantage of time, Henry was more objective than earlier authors, but he did not draw any new conclusions.

Other books that have valuable insights are those written by the men who rode with Forrest or knew him. They include John Watson Morton's *The Artillery of Nathan Bedford Forrest's Cavalry* (Nashville Publishing House of the M. E. Church, South, 1909) and William Witherspoon's *Reminiscences of a Scout, Spy and Soldier of Forrest's Cavalry* (Jackson, Tenn.: McCowat Mercer Printing Co., 1910). Dozens of books document the battles in which Forrest participated. The most valuable is Edwin C. Bearss's *Forrest at Brice's Cross Roads and in Northern Mississippi in 1864* (Dayton, Ohio: Morningside Bookshop, 1979).

The two best books on Forrest are the most recent: Brian Steel Wills's *A Battle from the Start: The Life of Nathan Bedford Forrest* (New York: HarperCollins, 1992) and Jack Hurst's *Nathan Bedford Forrest: A Biography* (New York: Alfred A. Knopf, 1993). Both authors have mined the primary and secondary sources to provide a complete and deeper understanding of Forrest and the controversies that surround him.

Also available in most large libraries are the published primary sources found in the *Official Records of the Union and Confederate Armies.* These volumes contain much of Forrest's wartime correspondence. Researchers may find dozens of other historical sketches and reminiscences in the *Confederate Veteran Magazine* and the *Southern Historical Society Papers.* Forrest's private papers can be found at Duke University, and letters relating to his activities are scattered in dozens of other institutions around the country.

Index

About the Author

Robert M. Browning Jr., Ph.D., is the chief historian of the U.S. Coast Guard. His previous books include *Success Is All That Was Expected: The South Atlantic Blockading Squadron during the Civil War; From Cape Charles to Cape Fear: The North Atlantic Blockading Squadron during the Civil War* (winner of the John Lyman Book Award and the Jefferson Davis Award); and *U.S. Merchant Vessel War Casualties of World War II*. He lives in Dumfries, Virginia.

MILITARY PROFILES
AVAILABLE

Farragut: America's First Admiral
Robert J. Scneller Jr.
Drake: For God, Queen, and Plunder
Wade G. Dudley
Santa Anna: A Curse upon Mexico
Robert L. Scheina
Eisenhower: Soldier-Statesman of the American Century
Douglas Kinnard
Semmes: Rebel Raider
John M. Taylor
Doolittle: Aerospace Visionary
Dik Alan Daso
Foch: Supreme Allied Commander in the Great War
Michael S. Neiberg
Villa: Soldier of the Mexican Revolution
Robert L. Scheina
Cushing: Civil War SEAL
Robert J. Schneller Jr.
Alexander the Great: Invincible King of Macedonia
Peter G. Tsouras
Rickover: Father of the Nuclear Navy
Thomas B. Allen and Norman Polmar
Forrest: The Confederacy's Relentless Warrior
Robert M. Browning Jr.
Meade: Victor of Gettysburg
Richard A. Sauers

MILITARY PROFILES
FORTHCOMING
Halsey
Robert J. Cressman
Tirpitz
Michael Epkenhans
Petain
Robert B. Bruce
Winfield Scott
Samuel Watson
Benedict Arnold
Mark Hayes